I0539114

The Wisdom Within

The Ancient Alchemy of Leadership

Stephen James

Council Leadership

Nashville, Tennessee

Front cover image and book design by
Circa Brand Agency.

Printed by IngramSpark® in the United States of America.

Printed October 2025.

Council Leadership
1010 Hardison Street
Nashville, Tennessee 37204

councilleadership.com

To members of
Council Leadership

When the Master governs, the people
Are hardly aware that he exists.
Next best is the leader who is loved.
Next, one who is feared.
The worst is one who is despised.

If you don't trust the people,
You make them untrustworthy.

The Master doesn't talk, he acts.
When his work is done,
The people say, "Amazing:
We did it, all by ourselves."

From the *Tao De Ching* by Lao Tzu

Translated by Stephen Mitchell

Contents

Introduction: 3,000,000,000 Words. ix

Chapter One: Leadership Alchemy
"The way forward lies within." 1

Chapter Two: The Warrior
"Life is meant to be hard." 17

Chapter Three: The Lover
"Relationship is essential." 37

Chapter Four: The King/Queen
"Control is an illusion." 55

Chapter Five: The Sage
"Everything is as it's intended." 71

Conclusion: Putting It Into Practice 85

Acknowledgments 91

Appendix A: Examples of the Four Archetypes 92

Appendix B: About Symbols 100

Appendix C: Supplemental Reading List 102

Endnotes 112

Introduction

3,000,000,000 Words.

At the time of this writing (2024), there are over 60,000 books on leadership for sale on Amazon. *Sixty thousand!* Meaning if a typical book contains 50,000 words, there are 3,000,000,000 words attempting to address the topic of leadership. *(3 billion!)* That's a lot of spilled ink. Why?

It's not rocket science.

Leadership is essential. Leadership is powerful. Leadership is meaningful. Leadership is dynamic, but leadership isn't rocket science. No, it's not. It's far more complicated. There's a whole lot to know in rocket engineering, but at the end of the day it adheres to knowable parameters rooted in the laws of physics. And while we may desire leadership to be as straightforward as rocket science, it is anything but.

When we try to make leadership something it's not, we further complicate an already difficult discipline. And sadly, that's what far too many of those three billion words are about. And while the intention to attempt to make something so complex as leadership clear and accessible is laudable, too often leadership gurus are starting from the wrong premise. Far too many of those books are trying to turn leadership into science instead of treating it for what it is: **artful human practice**. The very reason it's not simple means it should not be overly simplified.

It's a way of being.

Leadership belongs more in the purview of humanities or gardening than it does the business schools. It's far more philosophical, spiritual, agrarian, and artistic than many of us are comfortable with. For leadership to be most generative, it must be understood for what it is . . . more as art than science . . . more as a discipline than a system . . . more practice than mastery . . . more as a way of life than a position.

Then there's the people's problem.

Perhaps the primary reason leadership is so challenging is that leadership is about people, and as we know, *people are complex, dynamic, inconsistent, diverse, and mysterious.* Sometimes they are awe-inspiring, sometimes a pain. Frankly, if it weren't for the people, leadership would be as simple and straightforward as many of those three billion words try to make it. The most effective way to lead people is to be better at leading yourself. That's why a key element of becoming a master in the art of leadership is knowing how to lead from the inside out. This kind of artful leadership is difficult to teach but remarkable to witness . . . and transformative to experience.

It's what you make it.

Leadership is many things. While it's a role to play and a title to bear, it's also much more. It's vital, rewarding, necessary, challenging, frustrating, and lonely. At its best, leadership is transformational, virtuous, and liberating. At its worst, it's used to perpetuate evil, abuse, and enslave. In this way, leadership exposes the leader's true nature. It's a mirror of a leader's own character—for better and worse.

The crossroads is always an opportunity.

For twenty years, in my work as a psychotherapist, I had the privilege of walking alongside people who found themselves at the crossroads of change. Most of those I worked with were high performers and leaders (licensed professionals, entrepreneurs, executives, professional athletes, and performing artists). These were people who had a drive to make an impact on the world, but despite their extraordinary drive, care, and expertise, they all had the same thing in common: They needed something to change—usually some fundamental way they understood themselves and behaved in the world. When they found their way into my office it was because they were at moments in their lives when circumstances beyond their control no longer allowed them to hide from, numb out, or ignore the complexity of their humanity. They found themselves on the cusp of either everything falling apart (or it already had) and/or something badly needing to be different.[1]

We all encounter these crossroads in life, where we need help crafting a new way of understanding ourselves; a fresh way of making meaning and finding purpose. We come to this place again and again recognizing that what got us here won't get us where we want to go (or at least anywhere different). *Crossroads are some of the most hopeful and daunting moments in life.* We must make choices and we don't really know where each road will lead us.

Leading with heart and purpose.

Over time, my solo private practice evolved. Around 2010 I began to imagine something more where a team of people-helpers could collaboratively do something more together than any of them could do alone. In 2014, with the help of others, I launched Sage Hill Counseling—a resilient group practice that continues to serve the Nashville community more than a decade later. We grew from one center to two to three to four. I was leading something much bigger and more complex than I ever imagined—and I was doing it rather poorly. I was out over my skis, losing sleep, gaining weight, and burning out. I was at my own crossroads.

I needed help. A friend recommended a program called Strategic Coach. It was helpful in so many ways. The clarity and optimism that Dan Sullivan and his team pour into entrepreneurs is remarkable. And as I started applying what I was learning to my life and business, I started seeing more clearly that there was something much deeper happening below the water line. In 2016 at a quarterly Strategic Coach session, I noticed that some of the deeper questions of life, leadership, meaning, purpose, and significance I was wrestling with resonated with many other participants as well. We were hungry for deeper truth. My personality, training, and experience allowed me to notice and name some things that other leaders were feeling but couldn't put into words. As my interests began to rapidly expand beyond psychotherapy and performance psychology into leadership and team dynamics, I went into research mode.

It wasn't long before I began devoting my curiosity and energy to understanding and creating heart-forward leadership development models that integrate the best practices from psychotherapy, theology, philosophy, art, and management.

In the fall of 2019, I began unwinding my therapy practice, and I turned the reins of Sage Hill Counseling over to two great leaders, Sarah Norris and Cresson Haugland. I focused my attention with the help of Scott Hearon on creating a leadership development company and boutique consultancy called Council Leadership[2], formerly The Leadership Lab, guided by seven core beliefs that grew out of my research:

---

1. The world and our families are desperate for full-hearted leaders.

2. We must lead ourselves first.

3. What got us here won't get us where we want to go.

4. Leadership is lonely & we can't lead alone.

5. When it comes to leadership, EQ > IQ.

6. Leadership is an art.

7. Leadership is a sacred calling, virtuous practice, and noble responsibility.

Then there was a global pandemic . . . and Ted Lasso.

Keeping a fledgling business that was predicated on leaders meeting in small, intimate groups, face-to-face during a global pandemic was hard, but it also gave me the space to keep learning and engaging leaders. What I found, through countless hours of reading, writing, and conversations with leaders, is that our culture is starved for better examples than what we've been given. It's why the world fell in love with the fictional American Football-turned-Premier League soccer coach, Ted Lasso.

At a time when we were all searching for better leadership, Ted Lasso's example hit home. The show wasn't just a hit because it entertained us; it resonated deeply because it offered a vision of leadership that's compassionate, curious, humble, hopeful, emotionally intelligent, and grounded in genuine human connection. Ted's approach wasn't about having all the answers—it was about caring for people, showing up with heart, and leading with optimism and empathy. His unshakable positivity reminded us that even in tough times, there's always room for hope, a message that felt especially vital during the challenges of the pandemic.

Ted Lasso also redefined what it means to be a leader by embracing vulnerability and prioritizing team. He showed us that real leadership comes from unity, collaboration, and the practice that we can always strive to grow. The show's blend of humor and heart struck a chord, reminding us that leadership is as much about inspiring others as it is about guiding them. *Ted Lasso* wasn't just a show; it was a cultural touchstone, offering an archetype for the kind of leadership we're all yearning for.

"Archetypes transcend, guiding us they do."

Everyone knows Yoda is the wise Jedi Master whose profound (albeit grammatically creative) questions lead to truth and light. Similarly, just one note of Darth Vader's theme song, and you know he has succumbed to darkness. For centuries, Grimm's Fairy Tales have taught children about characters like Little Red Riding Hood, the archetype of innocence lost, who learns the hard lesson that not all creatures can be trusted. The Greek myths, like Icarus, who ignored his father's warnings, flew too close to the sun, and fell into the sea, are other examples. The Jewish and Christian Bibles are full of stories as well. David, chosen despite his unremarkable appearance and position as the youngest brother, rises above challenges to defeat Goliath. Jacob, wrestling with The Man in the dark of night, earns a blessing that comes with a disabling limp. These characters are archetypes, carrying universal meanings that transcend time, culture, and religion.[3]

I first encountered the concept of archetypes in a freshman English class at Belmont University in 1991 and was immediately drawn to the idea that humans are more alike than we are different. Years later, in graduate school (2001-2003) at The Seattle School for Theology and Psychology (formerly Mars Hill Graduate School), I reencountered the concept while exploring Carl Jung's writings, particularly *Man and His Symbols.* Jung believed archetypes are universal symbols or patterns that reside in the collective unconscious, shared by all humanity. These patterns manifest in myths, stories, dreams, and behaviors across cultures and time periods.

Later, I learned about Marie-Louise von Franz,[4] a key figure in Jungian psychology who expanded Jung's ideas on archetypes and personal transformation. She focused on how ancient myths, fairy tales, and alchemy reveal universal truths about human nature. Her studies of fairy tales showed how archetypes guide us through life's challenges. These stories aren't just entertainment; they offer timeless lessons in courage, compassion, power, and wisdom.

Von Franz believed alchemy symbolized personal transformation —not just turning lead into gold but refining our own struggles into strength and wisdom. This mirrors the journey of leadership, which is less about strategy and more about ongoing self-growth. Her exploration of individuation, or becoming your truest self, deeply resonates with leadership. True leadership, like individuation, isn't about external mastery—it's about knowing yourself and leading from within. *By embracing these archetypal forces, leaders can transform not just their actions but their entire way of being.*

Archetypal wisdom resonates.

While Jung wrote about numerous archetypes, the specific configuration of the King, Warrior, Magician, and Lover was later developed by Robert Moore and Douglas Gillette in a book of the same title as a way to understand and explore modern masculine psychology. Inspired by Moore and Gillette's clarity, Dane Anthony and I designed and facilitated an experiential men's retreat around these concepts around 2010. In this season, I also read a book by Fr. Richard Rohr called *Adam's Return*, which lays out his own version of archetypes, in preparation for writing *Wild Things: The Art of Nurturing Boys* with David Thomas. In it, we introduce a developmental model of boyhood broken down into five stages, each associated with a specific archetype: The Explorer (2-4 years old), The Lover (5-8 years old), The Individual (9-12 years old), The Wanderer (13-17 years old), The Warrior (18-22 years old). Fifteen years later, *Wild Things* continues to sell well and offers a deep dive into the unique developmental stages of boyhood, providing insights and actionable advice for parents, educators, and caregivers. Much of its popularity and power stem from its archetypal framework.

From a flash of wisdom, a leadership model emerged.

It's humbling and surprising how things come together sometimes, like a mixing pot in the background, combining all I'd been reading and learning about leadership and archetypes. Then, in the fall of 2022, I was hit with a wave of wisdom, a spark that ignited a flash of awareness and insight. What started as a short essay for Council Leadership grew into something more. The next two years (2023-2024) was dedicated to honing, sorting, polishing, and expanding. As I wrote and thought about this material, I saw how illuminating and encouraging it was for the members in Council Leadership. Through research and practice, I discovered a framework as enlightening as it is helpful and as simple as it is challenging: The Inner Council of Wisdom.

Let's begin.

As you begin this exploration into the wisdom of archetypes, understand that this isn't a paint-by-numbers approach; it's an ongoing, dynamic interplay of powerful, mystical forces. When you learn to listen to The Inner Council of Wisdom, you'll discover the clarity to lead with conviction and the compassion to connect with others. This work isn't simple, but it's deeply meaningful, guiding you into your own wisdom.

Leadership Alchemy

"The way forward lies within."

Life's a lot more mysterious than it seems at first glance. Beneath the daily grind—beneath the stress, the achievements, the never-ending to-do lists—there's a hidden world at play.

This world's ancient, powerful, and not easy to explain. For at least 95,000 years, humans have been crafting rituals, creating symbols, and spinning myths to tap into something bigger, something timeless. These rituals and myths hold universal truths, ones that cut across cultures, ages, and genders, crystallizing into what we call archetypes. Archetypes aren't just abstract concepts; they're deeply ingrained patterns that shape how we see ourselves and the world around us. And here's the kicker—they're crucial for leadership too. When leaders tap into these archetypes, they ground themselves in a wisdom that transcends the latest trends and fads. It's about digging deeper, connecting with a truth that's as old as time itself, and leading from that place of profound awareness.

See Beyond the Obvious, Lead with Depth

Wise, compassionate, and effective leadership isn't about following a formula, it's about practicing archetypal energies. *The Wisdom Within* explores leadership through The Inner Council of Wisdom, which is comprised of four core archetypes: The Warrior, The Lover, The King/Queen, and The Sage. These are powerful forces that reveal truths hidden in plain sight. This isn't just about making decisions—it's about seeing beyond the obvious, tapping into a deeper understanding that can transform your leadership. Engaging these archetypes puts us on a path to becoming effective, wise, insightful, and genuinely inspiring leaders.

The Warrior, Lover, King/Queen, and Sage aren't just abstract ideas—they're like raw materials in alchemy, shaping and refining us as we face the real challenges of leadership. Leadership isn't about just checking boxes or making surface-level moves. It's a journey of self-discovery, where these archetypal forces work to mold who we are and how we lead. In *The Wisdom Within*, we dig into how these archetypes can unlock real transformation. They're not just concepts—they're dynamic forces that, when tapped into, can change everything. By paying attention to your Inner Council of Wisdom, you start to see how each archetype shapes your decisions, your behavior, and the way you see the world. As you learn to recognize and balance these forces, you'll not only become more self-aware, but also lead with greater emotional intelligence and authenticity.

Seeing Archetypes from Every Angle

The Warrior, Lover, King/Queen, and Sage aren't just static roles—they're dynamic, multi-dimensional forces that operate on several levels at once. But here's the catch: black-and-white thinking, oversimplification, and linear approaches keep us from grasping their depth. Think of each archetype like a precious jewel. To truly understand the wisdom they offer, we need to examine them from seven different angles.

As we turn these archetypes in the light, we'll see how they sharpen our perspective and bring clarity to the complex realities we face.[5]

THE SEVEN FACETS

01
PHASES

02
POSTURES

03
POWERS

04
PRACTICES

05
FULFILLMENTS

06
DISTORTIONS

07
CONTEMPLATION

Facet 1: Phases

The simplest way to get a grip on these archetypes is to view them as a developmental path. Think of it as a loose timeline, where each archetype tends to be most accessible during certain seasons of life, but don't get too hung up on rigid boundaries. These phases aren't set in stone—sometimes they overlap, and sometimes they get stunted. Everyone's journey is different, and while each phase has its own traits, how we move through them varies widely.

Here's how it generally breaks down:

- **The Warrior:** 15–40 years

- **The Lover:** 25–50 years

- **The King/Queen:** 40–65 years

- **The Sage:** 50–75+ years

You'll notice there's a lot of overlap between these phases. That's because transitioning from one archetype to the next isn't always smooth. It takes time, and growth isn't always a straight line. We might circle back to earlier archetypes as new challenges or opportunities arise. This framework embraces the messy, nonlinear nature of personal development, reminding us that each stage brings its own wisdom and opportunities for transformation.

Another key takeaway is that these four phases are part of a bigger story. Drawing from Richard Rohr's insights, life's journey can be split into two major seasons: the First Journey and the Second Journey.[6]

The First Journey is all about building a strong and secure sense of identity. It's the season in life when you feel like you've got the whole world ahead of you, and you're busy laying down the foundations of who you are. This is where you're focused on external achievements, roles, and relationships—everything that helps you define yourself. Rohr calls this building the "container" of your life, the structure that'll later hold the deeper parts of your spiritual journey.

This season is all about two key things:

- **Establishing Identity:** You're shaping a coherent sense of self through your accomplishments, status, and the recognition you get from others. It's about setting those personal, professional, and social boundaries, and strengthening your Ego to navigate the world and make your mark.

- **Building Structure:** You're establishing order, stability, and security through your career, family, and societal contributions.

But here's the twist: *life has a way of shaking up that security, pushing you to search for something deeper.* That's when the possibility of a Second Journey opens—a journey that's no longer about achievement and success, but about digging deeper to find a truer, more grounded sense of self, meaning, and purpose.

The Second Journey usually kicks in during the midlife and shifts your focus from external achievements to internal transformation. Time starts to feel more precious, and you move from striving for success to seeking significance, from looking for external validation to finding inner fulfillment. This is the phase where you start to see failures, losses, and challenges not as setbacks, but as necessary portals for growth and transformation. It's about selectively emptying the "container" you built in the first journey and filling it with the contents of a more authentic, compassionate, and spiritually rich life.

This season is marked by:

- **Inner Exploration:** Turning inward to explore your inner world, motivations, and deeper truths. Letting go of the Ego's need for control, validation, and external success to embrace a more authentic and humble self.

- **Making Meaning:** Pursuing deeper meaning and purpose beyond material and social achievements. This is where you integrate the lessons and experiences of the first journey into a more holistic and mature spirituality. It's about accepting the complexities and contradictions of life, recognizing that true wisdom often lies in holding opposing truths in tension.

Midlife—roughly a third of your adult life—becomes that crucial passage where you transform from who you were into who you're meant to be.

The following illustration combines ideas of the four archetypes with Rohr's First and Second Journeys.

ARCHETYPES & JOURNEYS

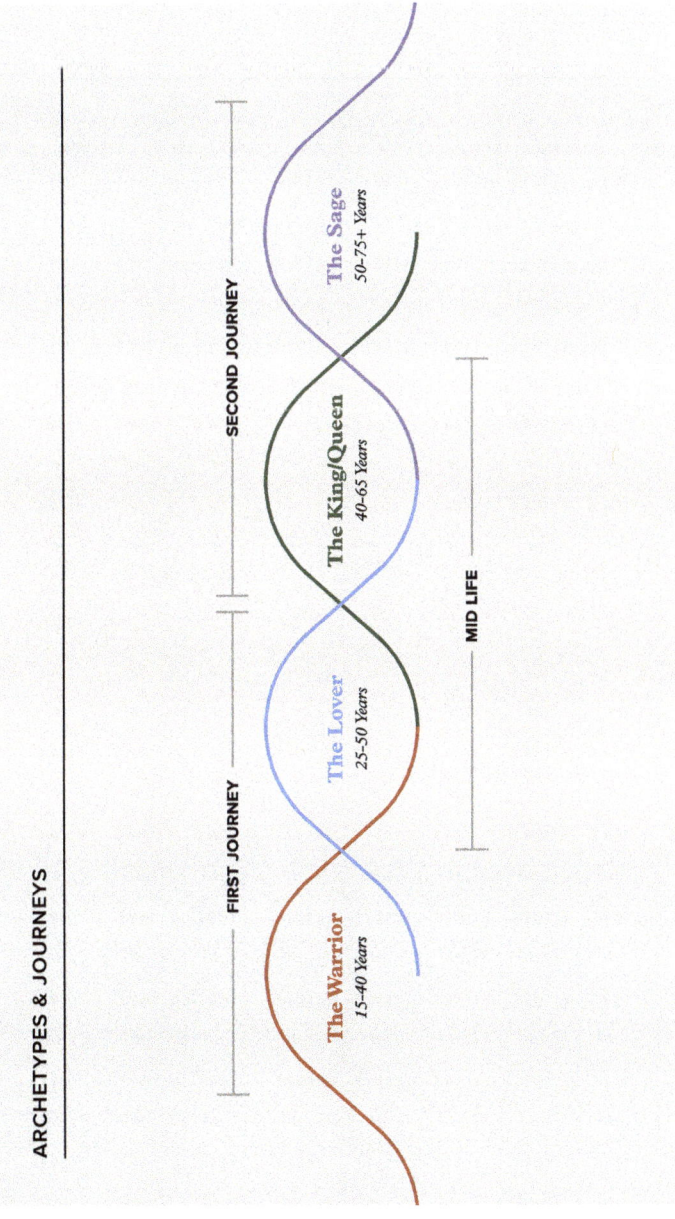

FIRST JOURNEY

SECOND JOURNEY

MID LIFE

The Warrior
15-40 Years

The Lover
25-50 Years

The King/Queen
40-65 Years

The Sage
50-75+ Years

WARNING: If you only see these four archetypes as developmental stages, you're missing out on most of their magic. Reducing them to just phases in life strips away their transcendence and seriously limits your ability to tap into their full power. Sure, looking at them developmentally can give us some insight, but if that's all you're doing, you're selling them—and yourself—short.

Just because you're in your 20s doesn't mean you're stuck with only Warrior energy. With a little practice, you can call any of these archetypes to the table, channeling the courage, loyalty, strength, or wisdom you need, right when you need it. You don't have to wait until you're 50 to start embodying the King, and you can absolutely cultivate Sage-like qualities in your 20s.

Think of it this way: these four archetypes come together to form your "Inner Council," a kind of round table of advisors that help you make decisions with your whole heart. Whether you're leading others or just trying to lead yourself, these archetypes are always there, ready to be called upon to guide you through whatever life throws your way.

Facet 2: Postures

Each archetype gives us a unique lens to view the world and engage with others. They shape how we understand things, influence our reactions, and determine our relationships. The way we read the world molds our thoughts, which then shape our actions—and it works the other way around too. Our actions reinforce and amplify our beliefs, attitudes, and behaviors, creating a feedback loop that makes the perspective we hold the key driver of how we think, act, and feel (identity.)

Facet 3: Powers

These archetypes aren't static—they're packed with living energy. Whether it's the Warrior's courage, the Lover's passion, the King/Queen's vision, or the Sage's contemplation, recognizing and tapping into these energies breathes life into our existence. When we do, our leadership transforms into a force of extraordinary effectiveness.

Facet 4: Practices

Each archetype comes with its own unique set of talents and skills, waiting to be cultivated. Awareness and practice are key—applying and adapting these skills is how we live in their benefit. By actively engaging with these practices, we can channel the courage, devotion, strength, or wisdom we need at any moment, empowering us to make full-hearted decisions and lead richer, more fulfilling lives.

Facet 5: Distorted Expressions

But here's the thing—each archetype has its shadows. If we're not careful, these shadows can twist and distort us. These are the ways in which the archetypes can show up in less developed, less beneficial forms in a leader's life. It's crucial to stay aware of these potential pitfalls, stumbling blocks, and malformations.

Facet 6: Fulfillment & Wisdom

The true promise of these archetypes is fulfillment, but you've got to take deliberate steps toward self-discovery and transformation to get there. The ongoing work of coming to grips with these realities—and sometimes getting knocked down by them or turned inside out—shows us that leadership is more than just professional growth. It's a vehicle for deep personal growth and possibly spiritual transformation. These archetypes guide leaders toward a more robust version of themselves by inviting them to four key truths of life:

- **The Warrior:** "Life is meant to be hard."

- **The Lover:** "Relationship is essential."

- **The King/Queen:** "Control is an illusion."

- **The Sage:** " Everything is as it's intended to be."

Facet 7: Contemplation (Digging Deeper)

At the end of each chapter, you'll find a set of questions designed to help you dig deeper into your own experience, insights, and awareness.

In the Appendix, you'll find examples of each archetype drawn from history, movies, books, and television. These examples are here to help you better understand what each archetype represents and to inspire you as you work on cultivating these traits in yourself.

When leaders tap into these archetypes, they begin a kind of personal alchemy, grounding themselves in a wisdom that transcends the latest trends and fads. It's about distilling something deeper, connecting with an ancient truth, and leading from that place of profound awareness and transformation.

A Holistic Approach

Knowing what each archetype brings to the table helps you live more intentionally. The Warrior pushes you to tackle challenges head-on, the Lover helps you build deep, meaningful connections, the King/Queen inspires you to lead with vision, and the Sage nudges you toward wisdom and generosity. The goal is to integrate these archetypes within yourself so you can draw on their strengths whenever needed. This holistic approach leads to a more balanced, dynamic way of leading, where you can navigate life's twists and turns with grace and resilience. By diving into these facets, you'll unlock the full potential of these archetypes, transforming both your life and leadership in powerful ways.

Each archetype brings its own vital strengths—the Warrior's courage, the Lover's compassion, the King/Queen's vision—but the real magic of agile leadership shines through under the guidance of the Sage. The Sage lets leaders channel and harmonize these forces, instinctively sensing how much courage, empathy, or vision is needed in any given moment. The Sage doesn't just balance these energies; it orchestrates them, weaving each archetype into a flexible, adaptive approach that meets the demands of any situation.

With the Sage as the guiding force, leaders become both agile and grounded, able to respond to challenges with greater clarity, depth, and perspective. This integration of archetypes creates a leadership style that's resilient and wise, turning the complexities of leadership into opportunities for deeper influence, purpose, and real change.

To get a truer sense of how these archetypes work together, picture them as three overlapping forces. Where the Warrior, Lover, and King/Queen meet, there exists something more: The Sage. This confluence is where each archetype blends into something wiser, more adaptable, and ultimately more powerful than any one alone. The Sage is the harmonizing force, bringing together the strengths of the other three and helping leaders be agile, grounded, and able to meet whatever comes their way. The illustration on the next page shows how the Sage most fully emerges at the convergence of courage, compassion, and vision.

HOW THE ARCHETYPES WORK TOGETHER

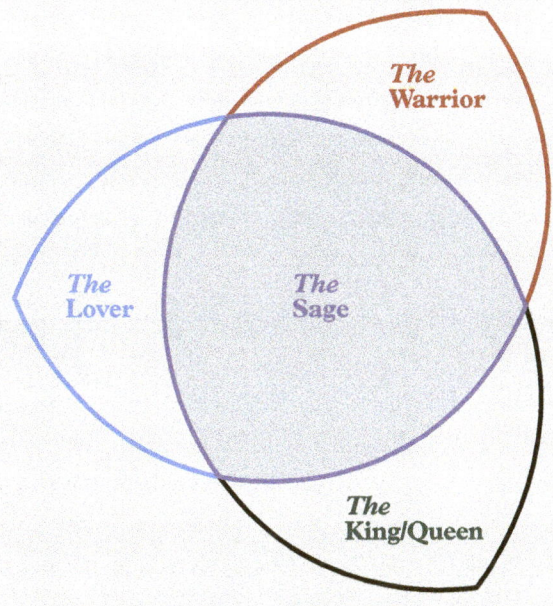

Practice Makes Useful

Admittedly, approaching this multidimensional framework of leadership from so many perspectives may seem complex, but it's precisely this complexity that makes the model so powerful. It's a dynamic, non-linear approach that adapts to the shifting demands of leadership. By embracing this layered, flexible framework, leaders can navigate challenges with greater wisdom, agility, and a deeper sense of purpose.

While the ideas in this book lean into mystical and contemplative traditions, they're basically useless without practical application. This book is a meditation for leaders and people helpers who take life seriously and want to lead and serve with emotional intelligence, self-awareness, and compassion, whether at home, at work, or in their communities.

You're invited to go inward, to recognize the different perspectives within you. When you tune into these archetypes, your internal dialogue shifts, fostering a balanced leadership style where each archetype finds its rightful place. Embracing this Inner Council of Wisdom allows you to navigate life's complexities with greater empathy, clarity, resilience, and authenticity. With time and practice, you can bring these perspectives into harmony and start leading from a place of deep connection and wisdom.

"

I realize that under the circumstances you have described you feel the need to see clearly. But your vision will become clear only when you can look into your own heart.

Without, everything seems discordant; only within does it coalesce into unity. Who looks outside dreams, who looks inside awakes.[7]

CARL JUNG

CHAPTER TWO

The Warrior

"Life is meant to be hard."

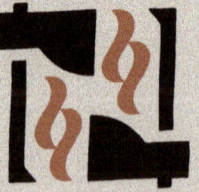

All cultures have Warriors who are the disciplined defenders of the Kingdom. Tough, singular in focus, and courageous, the Warrior is willing to put their own life on the line for the sake of the kingdom and the glory that comes with either victory or death (or the shame that comes with defeat). It's hard to imagine a civilization lasting without the presence of highly trained warriors.

In Greek mythology, Heracles, or Hercules as the Romans knew him, is hailed as one of the greatest heroes. His life was a relentless series of epic feats, driven by a quest for redemption and immortality.

Heracles had a tangled family tree. Born from Zeus, the king of gods, and Alcmene, a mortal woman, Heracles was marked from the start with incredible strength and courage. But Zeus's wife, Hera, was furious—rightly so, considering Zeus's notorious affairs. When Heracles was just an infant, Hera sent two snakes to kill him in his crib. But baby Heracles, strong and fearless, choked the snakes before they could strangle him.

Hera's vendetta didn't stop there. She cursed Heracles with a life of endless trials. In a fit of rage driven by her spell, he once killed his beloved wife and children. Consumed by guilt, Heracles sought out Apollo, the god of truth and healing (and another of Zeus's offspring), and begged for punishment.

Apollo, knowing that Hera's rage was behind Heracles's madness, didn't dismiss him but set him on a path of atonement. He ordered Heracles to complete twelve daunting labors for

King Eurystheus of Mycenae. If Heracles succeeded, Apollo promised he'd be cleansed of his guilt and granted immortality.

The Twelve Labors weren't just about showing off strength; they were Heracles's journey to redemption. Each task tested his bravery, resourcefulness, and endurance. Heracles wasn't after mere glory. He was fighting against overwhelming odds to make amends and earn his place among the gods. This is nowhere clearer than in his last trial: **The Capturing of Cerberus.**[8]

Cerberus wasn't just any beast. Born from Titans, he boasted three heads, a serpent's tail, and snakes writhing down his back. Guarding the gates of the Underworld, he was a living barricade. No soul could slip past, and no living soul could cross into his realm without Hades's say-so.

Heracles had a monumental task ahead: capture Cerberus and drag him up from the depths. The Underworld was no place for the living, but Heracles wasn't one to back down. He'd fought many fights, but this was different. This was a plunge into the heart of darkness.

Heracles trudged into the Underworld, burdened by the enormity of his mission. He met Hades and requested the right to seize Cerberus. Hades, recognizing the fire in Heracles's eyes, gave his nod.

Facing Cerberus was no small feat. The beast was a nightmare—three heads snapping, a tail thrashing, and serpents hissing. But Heracles was resolved. He went to work, using every ounce of his strength and cunning to subdue the monster. It was a grueling battle, but Heracles prevailed, binding Cerberus without delivering a fatal blow.

Dragging Cerberus to the surface, Heracles brought the beast into the light. The sight was as terrifying as expected. Cerberus was a force of dread, underscoring the grim realities of the world beyond. Heracles's aim wasn't to cause more fear but to demonstrate his might and resolve.

When Heracles presented Cerberus to Eurystheus, the king was visibly shaken. Heracles had not only met but exceeded the challenge. He'd wrestled with the beast of the Underworld and won.

Once the task was done, Heracles returned Cerberus to his rightful place. The beast resumed his role, keeping watch over the line between life and death.

Heracles' choice to return Cerberus to Hades rather than destroy him is layered with symbolic meaning, offering profound insights into leadership, restraint, and the nature of power. This act transcends mere physical might or the subjugation of a monstrous adversary; it speaks to the deeper wisdom of recognizing when to harness strength and when to release it.[9]

1. Respect for Boundaries

Cerberus, as the guardian of the Underworld, has a necessary role. By returning him, Hercules acknowledges the importance of maintaining balance rather than asserting dominance. True leadership often means preserving what must endure.

2. Power with Purpose

Heracles, known for his brute strength, reveals a new form of power: restraint. Capturing Cerberus without killing him shows that real strength lies in using power wisely—to preserve rather than destroy.

3. Mastery of Self

This labor is as much about internal mastery as external victory. By sparing Cerberus, Heracles conquers his own aggression and pride, choosing restraint over conquest.

4. Strength and Humility

To descend into the Underworld and return Cerberus unharmed is an act of humility. Heracles honors Hades' domain, showing that leadership sometimes means submitting to a higher order.

5. Acceptance of Mortality

Cerberus symbolizes death, the boundary between life and the afterlife. Heracles respects that boundary, recognizing that death is not an enemy to vanquish but a reality to honor.

6. Wisdom Gained

In myth, the hero's journey ends not with brute force but with transformation. By returning Cerberus, Heracles emerges wiser, embodying a heroism defined by balance and respect rather than sheer might.

Heracles' final labor, then, is as much about psychological integrity and inner mastery as it is about physical might. This choice to preserve rather than destroy marks his transformation from a warrior into something more—one who wields power with restraint, wisdom, and respect for the greater order.

Spring Break: 1987

In the summer of 1987, when I was fourteen, my family packed up the car and headed to Destin in the Florida Panhandle for Spring Break. I was on the brink of a milestone—about to get my learner's permit. I was craving independence and excited for the trip, secretly hoping to meet a girl from some other southern city like Atlanta or Birmingham. My parents let me bring my road bike. In my teenage mind's eye I was kinda picturing a John Hughes movie of which I was the lead. (Hoping to be seen as a Kevin Bacon or Emilio Estevez type guy though in reality I was much more of Michael J. Fox or Anthony Michael Hall.)

Back then, I'd gotten into road biking and had a steel blue Centurion LeMans RS 12-Speed and all the gear: bike shorts, jerseys, gloves, those fancy shoes that clipped in (which was a big deal in the late '80s), and water bottles. I even had a "bike computer"—a fancy digital speedometer/odometer. I'm still not sure how we managed to fit the bike into the car.

A few days in, I set off on my bike for Panama City Beach, about thirty miles from our place in Destin. The ride started easy and fast. The warm wind was at my back, and I could taste the salt in the air. I felt powerful, averaging over 25mph on the way there.

The ride back was a different story. A few miles in, it was like I was riding through syrup. The wind that had pushed me east was now slamming into my face. The humidity thickened, and the midday sun beat down hard. Every pedal stroke was a struggle. Total misery. What had I gotten myself into? Twenty-seven miles to go. Twenty-six. Twenty-five and a half. Twenty-four. Miles were slow. Out of water, my digital speedometer seemed to taunt me. Should I quit? Could I make it back? Should I pull over and hope for a rescue? Just keep going?

Three hours later, I finally made it back to the condo. I was wiped out, thirsty, a bit wiser, and badly sunburned—neck, calves, forearms, and a bright red oval on each hand where my gloves didn't cover. I'd been bold and reckless, sure, but I'd pushed through. I felt like I had done something.

Both the tale of Heracles and my 1987 bike ride are an unfiltered truth: facing tough challenges head-on and refusing to back down, no matter how tough things get. Heracles, that legendary Greek hero, tackled twelve grueling labors. Each one pushed him to his limits, but the ultimate test was capturing Cerberus, the three-headed beast guarding the Underworld. This wasn't just about muscle; it was about guts, determination, and facing the darkest fears to claw his way to redemption.

My bike ride from Destin to Panama City Beach was my own Herculean test. I started with a sense of adventure, daydreaming about the journey ahead, only to slam into a wall of struggle and exhaustion. The wind that once carried me now punched me in the face, and the sun seemed hell-bent on roasting me alive. Every mile became a battle, each pedal stroke a hard-won victory. This wasn't about looking good or proving something to anyone else. It was about facing my own demons—pushing myself to the limit and finding out what I was really made of. The lesson? It's not about avoiding the hard stuff; it's about meeting it head-on and pushing through.

Have you been there, facing down those moments when the wind's against you, and you've got to dig deep just to keep moving? That's the Warrior in us. Think of Rocky Balboa running up those steps, or Simone Biles making her epic comeback, cementing her place as the GOAT. History's full of legends like Spartacus, Leonidas, Joan of Arc, and Genghis Khan—showing us what passion, endurance, and grit look like.

Phase

As part of life's arc, the Warrior's core attributes begin to emerge around 13-16 years old and intensify throughout a person's twenties and through their early thirties. It's the Warrior archetype that helps us find a context where a person can *show up, step up,* and *set themselves apart.* During this transformative phase, the Warrior empowers us to find our place, seize opportunities, and distinguish ourselves as we effort to chisel our identity from the stone of our personality, skill set, culture, and circumstance.

Posture

Whether we know it or not, the Warrior compels us to strive for confidence, achievement, and success in effort to tackle deep questions connected to self-worth, shame, anxiety, and insecurity. *The Warrior teaches us that pain can be a path to growth and righteousness, though it also warns us of pointless suffering.*

Relationally, the Warrior archetype will lead us to see others as rivals or enemies causing us to navigate the world in absolutes of either/or, good/bad, and black/white terms. It's this archetype that helps us be purposeful, prepared, disciplined, austere, decisive, and skilled, but below the surface, the Warrior keeps us largely emotionally, spiritually, and psychologically underdeveloped and relationally unavailable. Relationally, the Warrior's strengths—discipline, decisiveness, and purpose—become barriers. Its focus on control and action overshadows emotional sensitivity, making it difficult to truly listen or engage vulnerably. What serves well in high-stake situations (like battle) transforms into emotional rigidity in relationships, keeping us distant, defensive, and quick to dominate and little room for nuance, empathy, or genuine connection.

Spiritually, the Warrior archetype fuels disciplines like fasting, chastity, sacrifice, secrecy, submission, and frugality (but only as right behavior). These disciplines provide a structure or place to invest time and energy into deepening the relationship with the Divine by providing a place for spiritual formation to take place and create a context in which one can come to the end of themselves and encounter GOD.

Psychologically, The Warrior archetype makes meaning in the world through winning and losing. It causes us to relate to ourselves and others (even GOD) through a framework of competition, achievement, and conquest. The heartbeat of a Warrior is victory, and the questions that live at the center of that struggle are: *"Do I have what it takes?"* and *"How can I find sure footing in the world?"*

"

The Warrior teaches us that pain can be a path to *growth and righteousness*, though it also warns us of *pointless suffering*.

Practice

The Warrior helps us acquire the technical skills to succeed in whatever station or situation in which we find ourselves, but beyond that the Warrior archetype gives us the strength of unyielding resolve. The Warrior archetype affords us a set of vital tools: discipline, practice, preparation, goal-setting, and submission to appropriate authority, but more than anything, *the Warrior helps us develop grit.*

Power

The Warrior propels us towards our objectives, inspiring us to champion noble causes. Warrior energy is colored by aggression, focus, and desire. It fuels the daily dedication and unwavering commitment needed to mold our futures into reality. It is the potent fuel of legacy. This spirit empowers leaders to persist unwaveringly toward distant goals; a stamina that sustains their vision through the ebb and flow of time.

Distorted Expressions

When ignored, undeveloped, or accessed with recklessness, the immature Warrior will lead you to take more than you give or provide less than you need. The immature Warrior reveals itself in several shadow forms.

- **The Showman** is the Warrior's shadow, craving the spotlight and driven by a need for glory and attention rather than purpose. Unlike the true Warrior, who fights for deeper principles, the Showman prioritizes image over substance, constantly seeking external validation and applause. The Showman is always performing, more concerned with how actions are perceived than with their true value. While the Showman might achieve moments of fame, these victories are fleeting and ultimately hollow, with a focus on the limelight often leads the Showman to lose sight of what really matters.

- **The Savior (Martyr)** shows up when a Warrior's craving for recognition takes over. He doesn't just want to win—he wants to be seen as a savior, placed on a pedestal of righteousness. This self-righteous drive, fueled by inner perfectionism, pushes him toward dangerous self-sacrifice and unnecessary suffering.

- **The Vigilante** tosses aside certain moral and ethical standards in the pursuit of what he sees as a "higher" form of justice. Unlike the true Warrior, who fights for a noble cause, the Vigilante adopts a Machiavellian mindset, where power is the goal, and the ends justify any means.

- **The Coward** avoids any internal or external conflict, clinging to a superficial kind of peace. When the pressure builds and the question "Do I have what it takes?" looms, the Coward doesn't stick around to find out. Instead, the Coward makes a snap judgment and decides he's not up to the task.

- In its most twisted forms, the Warrior becomes **the Sadist** or **the Masochist** who lead us to being cruel either to others or to ourselves. As Carl Jung described, the Sadist is cruel, even to those closest to them, with contempt for weakness. The Masochist, on the other hand, feels powerless, letting others exploit them, often without realizing it.

Fulfillment

By embracing this archetype, leaders tap into a deep well of inner strength, grit, and the determination to fight for what's worth fighting for. The Warrior helps leaders find their highest calling in serving something bigger than oneself—pursuing missions that go beyond personal glory. It energizes leaders to create and commit to causes that matter, ones that demand sacrifice and push them beyond their comfort zones. The Warrior helps leaders clarify who they are, stick to their path with discipline, and face challenges with unshakable resolve.

The Warrior enables leaders to face, accept, and internalize the reality that *"Life is meant to be hard."* This reality is not a burden for the Warrior; rather, it is the very anvil upon which their resilience, character, and courage are formed.

The Warrior helps leaders find a grounding force, a reminder that true strength is born not in the absence of difficulty, but in the heart of it. This realization shapes an approach to leadership that is unafraid to confront and endure hardships. It teaches that the path of true leadership is often strewn with obstacles, and it is in navigating these with courage and resolve that a leader's mettle is truly tested and proven. This understanding of life's inherent struggles does not dampen the Warrior spirit; rather, it enlivens it, imbuing their leadership with an authenticity and depth that can only come from a deep engagement with life's most challenging realities.

Luke Skywalker in the Trenches . . . but without the Force.

In 2023, I was in Iceland, leading a leadership development trip with Council Leadership and Wilderness Collective. We were on a weeklong KTM dual sport motorcycle adventure around the Golden Circle in southern Iceland. My role that day was to be the "Tail"—the experienced rider who hangs back, ready to help if needed and make sure no one gets left behind. The guy in front of me was all over the trail, making it tough to keep my own ride steady. So I pulled over, gave him some space, and took in the breathtaking scenery. The trail ran along one side of a glacial valley, covered in dark volcanic sand, with massive volcanic rocks flanking both sides. Towering mountains loomed around us. It was a perfect day to ride.

After about fifteen minutes, I got back on my bike, feeling relaxed and ready to roll. Bit by bit, I started picking up speed. I was in the zone—hitting little jumps, pushing myself faster and faster. As I zipped along the trail, I felt like Luke Skywalker flying through the Death Star trenches, fully locked in and unstoppable. That was until I ran into the force—the force of gravity.

I hit a jump—way too fast, way too hard—and didn't stick the landing. My bike and I parted ways, and I went tumbling through the air, spinning heels over head, landing about twenty feet down the trail.

The impact was brutal. My helmet cracked. My vision blurred. I couldn't move, couldn't breathe. The pain was intense. My first thought? I'd broken my back, and I was dying. But after several seconds, I managed to gasp for air and realized I'd just knocked the wind out of myself. I lay there under the gray Icelandic sky, terrified and in serious pain. I wiggled my toes and fingers, moved my head from side to side. I tried to get my gloves off and remove my helmet but couldn't do either. Rolling over onto all fours, I felt like I was going to puke.

A few minutes later, Griff and Johnny—the Wilderness trip partners who were there to shoot video and photos—found me and helped me get my bearings. They looked concerned. I was equal parts relieved and humiliated. I was supposed to be the guy helping and leading others, and here I was, on my hands and knees on a dirt road in Iceland, barely able to move.

Not long after, the lead guide found us. We were about two hours from our hotel and three from the nearest medical center. If something was seriously wrong, I was in trouble. We figured my best bet was to ride out if I could, rather than wait around. They helped me back on my bike, which, miraculously, still worked fine. It hurt like hell, and I could only stand—not sit—but I could ride. Or at least I thought I could, until I wrecked again just a few meters down the trail. I was shaken up. They helped me back on the bike a second time, and we started off to catch up with the rest of the group. Adrenaline at full peg I rode the next couple of hours eventually making it back to the hotel.

Long story short, after a shower, half a beer, and fainting in the lobby, I found myself in a van headed to the hospital. I wanted to ride out to the peak of an incredible vista, but instead, I ended up in an Icelandic E.R. After some X-rays, MRIs, and ultrasounds, I found out I only had a few broken ribs and some pretty nasty nerve damage in my lower back. A handful of pain meds and a few days of rest would do me some good.

Thankfully, my back wasn't broken, but I took a hit to my pride—and the irony wasn't lost on me. My own reckless Warrior energy got me into this mess, and that same Warrior grit got me out.

Where Growth Meets Grit

All Warriors take hits, and in the end, those scars are proof of their strength and resilience. Picture a medical resident grinding through endless hours in school and at the hospital, all for the worthy goal of becoming a doctor. Or think of a single mom, burning the midnight oil at night school to create a better life for herself and her kids. What keeps her pushing forward? There's a reason we say someone is fighting cancer—when life and death are on the line, we're forced to dig deep, tapping into a well of inner strength and fortitude to claim victory. In these, and countless other battles in life, people must channel their inner Warrior.

Strength in Struggle

The Warrior archetype is a vital part of any leader's inner wisdom. At its best, the Warrior offers leaders a deep well of inner strength, empowering them to commit to a virtuous cause or even sacrifice for something greater than their own success or reputation. Tapping into this energy, the Warrior provides the courage needed to champion the Mission.

True Warriors remind us that life isn't meant to be easy—most of it's hard. *True strength of character isn't born from avoiding difficulty, but from developing the courage to confront it head-on.* This understanding shapes an approach to leadership, one that doesn't shy away from challenges but meets them with optimism and resolve.

The Warrior archetype isn't just about brute strength or facing down epic challenges; it's about the pursuit of growth, purpose, and resilience. Life's meant to be hard, and that's not something to shy away from. It's in contending the moments when you encounter your limits that you find out more of who you are and what you're made of. The Warrior within us reminds us that resilience comes from the practice of facing the tough stuff, not from avoiding it. Whether you're leading a team, chasing a dream, or just trying to make it through a rough patch, remember that the Warrior's heartbeat is victory—and that victory is earned, not given.

"

Do not pray for an easy life; pray for the strength to endure a difficult one.

BRUCE LEE

Key Takeaways and Insights:

- **The Warrior's Journey:** True strength isn't just about physical prowess; it's about confronting and overcoming the most difficult challenges life throws our way.

- **Resilience and Redemption:** Like Heracles, the path to redemption and personal growth often involves enduring and overcoming significant trials.

- **Facing Fears:** The Warrior archetype teaches that life's hardships are not burdens but opportunities to forge resilience, courage, and perseverance.

- **Leadership Through Struggle:** Effective leadership is cultivated through navigating tough circumstances with resolve, not by avoiding difficulties.

- **Balanced Warrior Energy:** While the Warrior's drive can push us forward, it must be tempered to avoid recklessness that can lead to harm.

Digging Deeper

- How do you connect with the Warrior's traits? Are there parts you lean into or push against?

- When have you seen the Warrior archetype really show up in your life?

- Looking back, can you tell when you were guided by the mature Warrior versus the immature one?

- How do you see the Warrior archetype playing into leadership, especially when it comes to sacrificing for something bigger than yourself?

- How do society's views on winning and losing shape your relationship with the Warrior archetype?

- Looking at the list of examples of Warrior leaders in Appendix A, which Warrior resonates with you the most, and why?

- Thinking about these leaders or others that come to mind driven by Warrior energy throughout history, what impact do you see that having the world around them?

- How can you channel the Warrior's energy for positive change, both in your life and in the world around you?

- Remember a time when you saw someone embody the Warrior archetype. How did that shape your view of them, and what did you take away from it?

- Can you think of any real-world or fictional examples where the immature Warrior shows up? How do these versions of the Warrior get in the way of the true potential and values of the archetype?

CHAPTER THREE

The Lover

"Relationship is essential."

Patient, kind, enduring, generous, and compassionate —the Lover archetype calls life into existence. With its boundless compassion, it can vanquish the darkest shadows of fear and shame. The Lover helps us find a context where we can reach out, open up, and share ourselves. To unlock its profound compassion, strength, and tenderness, we must recognize, nurture, and master its essence.

One iconic example of The Lover in modern times is J.R.R. Tolkien's character Samwise Gamgee from *The Lord of the Rings* trilogy books and movies. Sam's unwavering loyalty, deep compassion, and selfless devotion to Frodo Baggins perfectly capture this archetype. Throughout their journey to destroy the One Ring, Sam's love for Frodo drives him to go to extraordinary lengths, often putting Frodo's needs above his own.

A humble gardener from the Shire, Sam is Frodo's steadfast companion on the perilous quest to destroy the One Ring. He's there for Frodo in the darkest moments, offering hope and support even when Frodo starts to lose faith. When Frodo is too weak to go on, Sam is determined to see their mission through. Sam's commitment isn't about seeking glory or recognition; it's fueled by his deep love for his friend, showing the transformative power of loyalty and sacrifice.

One of the most poignant moments in which Sam embodies The Lover archetype is when he carries Frodo up Mount Doom. As they near the end of their grueling journey, Frodo is utterly exhausted, drained both physically and emotionally by the burden of the One Ring. Seeing his friend in this state,

Sam says, "I can't carry it for you, but I can carry you." Then, he lifts Frodo onto his shoulders and carries him up the treacherous slopes.

This moment perfectly captures the Lover archetype as Sam's deep empathy and selflessness push him beyond his limits for Frodo's sake. His love for Frodo drives his determination to finish the mission, no matter what it takes. Sam's not after glory; he's motivated purely by his devotion to Frodo and their shared cause. Carrying Frodo up that mountain shows how the Lover archetype channels emotional depth, compassion, and sacrifice into transformative action.

The Compassionate Architects of Human Flourishing

To understand the Lover archetype in leadership is to recognize those who serve not with power but with presence—those whose very way of being creates opportunities for the growth, healing, and belonging of others. This kind of leadership isn't always found on stages or in titles. It is often felt rather than seen— quiet, faithful, and transformative.

Fred Rogers, beloved creator of *Mister Rogers' Neighborhood*, led with a heart attuned to the emotional landscapes of children. His television program was not just entertainment—it was a sanctuary. In a world often loud and indifferent, Rogers offered gentle language, silence, and eye contact as a way to tell children they were seen, valued, and safe. His leadership was an act of sacred listening. He mentored not through instruction, but through presence—inviting children (and adults alike) into self-acceptance and emotional honesty. He modeled a way of leading that prioritizes tenderness over tactics, connection over control.

Maria Montessori, physician and educational pioneer, shaped her entire pedagogy around the innate dignity and potential of the child. She didn't seek to mold students into achievers; she sought to unearth the person already within. Her classrooms became environments of quiet revolution—spaces marked by order, beauty, and autonomy where children could explore, make mistakes, and experience the joy of self-directed learning. Montessori's leadership reflected a Lover's vision: she saw not just what was but what could be. She elevated learning to its rightful place as a relational, human, and soulful endeavor.

Then there's Jean Vanier, who founded the L'Arche communities—spaces where people with and without intellectual disabilities live together in mutual care. Vanier's leadership began not with vision statements, but with vulnerability. He chose to live alongside those the world often marginalized, and in doing so, he redefined power as proximity. His leadership was marked not by personal achievement, but by what he made possible for others. He believed that the deepest form of leadership is to invite others into a life of communion, where we are not just helpers or helped, but companions on the journey toward becoming fully human.

Each of these leaders reminds us that the Lover archetype is not sentimental or soft—it is powerful and inspiring. It takes courage to stay open, to nurture others without demanding control, and to hold space for growth that can't be hurried. The Lover as leader nourishes what longs to grow, heals what has been harmed or neglected, listens for what longs to be heard, and honors what's often overlooked. In their own ways, Rogers, Montessori, and Vanier reveal that to lead with love is not to be passive—it is to be profoundly awake, deeply rooted, and radically committed to the flourishing of others.

Phase

The Lover archetype starts emerging in the early to mid-twenties, gaining prominence throughout the late twenties and into the late thirties. During this season of life, the Lover teaches us to collaborate, be vulnerable, and express ourselves. It leads us to find a place where we can reach out, open up, and share who we are with the world. It's the Lover that compels us to reach out, reveal our authentic selves, and engage with others not just for what they can give us, but for the shared experience of being truly seen and known. This archetype teaches us that connection is not just an external pursuit—it's an internal transformation that shapes who we are, revealing layers of beauty, creativity, and sensitivity.

Posture

The Lover archetype helps us navigate life through creativity, negotiation, collaboration, and compromise. *The Lover is more the posture of a mother nurturing a child than it is of a passionate romantic.* It sees the world in win/win, we/us, and both/and terms, and it connects us to the world through our senses—smell, taste, touch, hearing, and sight. The Lover drives us to engage in relationships with a sense of reciprocity, inviting us to see others as partners and collaborators. It draws us into relationships by acknowledging not just our own vulnerability and neediness, but also those of others. This fuels our empathy, giving us insight into people and situations, and helping us build rapport quickly. But the Lover also knows that giving your heart fully to anyone or anything means embracing the inevitability of heartbreak.

Relationally, The Lover is all about connection. It's the force that makes meaning in the world through creativity, negotiation, collaboration, and compromise. The Lover archetype drives us to connect and engage relationships with reciprocity. It helps us see others as partners, compatriots, and collaborators. It draws us into relationships through acknowledging our own vulnerability and neediness and the vulnerability and neediness of others. It fuels empathy that gives us insight into others and situations as well as the ability to read people and build rapport quickly.

Psychologically, The Lover makes us emotionally sensitive and attuned to ourselves and others. Deep questions swirl in the Lover's heart: *Am I alone? Will anyone have me? Do you like me? Do I like me? Can I receive another? Can I give myself to another?* Idealistic and passionate, the Lover seeks connection, collaboration, and communion, but its heartbeat is often loneliness and desire, drawing forth deep longings that can't be fully fulfilled.

Spiritually, the Lover archetype nurtures our connection to the divine, fostering a deep sense of devotion, adoration, and worship. Embracing this archetype opens us up to a world of signs, omens, intuition, and premonitions, where the unseen becomes just as real as the tangible. The Lover leans into the tension between emptiness and fullness, recognizing that each is incomplete without the other. This archetype fuels our spiritual journey, guiding us to find meaning in the spaces between, and teaching us that true spiritual growth comes from embracing both the presence and absence of what we seek.

Practice

The Lover, brimming with vulnerability, insight, curiosity, patience, and service, guides us in the art of meaningful exchange with others. It's not just about transactions or surface-level interactions; it's about truly understanding and connecting with people in ways that lead to mutual benefit. The Lover teaches us to be open, to give and receive with a full heart, knowing that the best exchanges are those where both parties walk away enriched, not just in material terms, but in emotional and spiritual growth as well.

In practice, the Lover archetype enables us to become skilled restorers, mending what's broken and nurturing what's been neglected. This isn't just about fixing things; it's about seeing the potential for wholeness even amid imperfection. *The Lover holds a vision of what things could be in their fullness—whether that's a relationship, a community, or a personal goal—while also accepting the reality of what they are today.* It's this balance between idealism and realism that allows the Lover to be a force of change, gently guiding us to create spaces where healing and growth can happen.

The Lover also encourages us to embrace the long game. It teaches us that restoration isn't always immediate; it's a process that requires patience, perseverance, and a willingness to sit with discomfort. The Lover knows that true change often comes slowly, through steady, consistent effort and a deep commitment to seeing things through. In this way, the Lover helps us cultivate resilience, not just in ourselves, but in those we interact with, creating environments where mutual benefit and shared growth are the norms rather than the exceptions.

"

The Lover holds a vision of what things could be in their *fullness*—whether that's a relationship, a community, or a personal goal—while also accepting the reality of what they are *today*.

Power

When we tap into the Lover's energy, we're driven by a desire for wholeness, beauty, and fulfillment. The Lover doesn't settle for half-measures—it wants to bring everything into harmony, creating a sense of completeness in both our internal and external worlds. This energy is all about loyalty, compassion, and inclusion, building spaces where tenderness, hospitality, acceptance, and forgiveness are the bedrock of our interactions.

The Lover archetype is a powerful source of creativity, pushing us beyond our fear and shame to express ourselves with a mix of imagination and vulnerability. Whether it's through painting, sculpture, poetry, music, theater, pottery, literature, or dance, the Lover fuels our artistic endeavors, encouraging us to explore and share our innermost thoughts and feelings. This creative energy isn't just about making art; it's about using creativity to connect with others and ourselves on a deeper level.

The real power of the Lover lies in how it transforms relationships. It gives us the perspective of mercy and grace, letting us approach others with empathy and curiosity. Instead of rushing to judgment, the Lover encourages us to see the world through compassionate eyes, understanding that everyone has their own story, struggles, and dreams. This mindset enriches our relationships, deepens connections, and builds trust. Through the Lover's energy, we find the courage to be vulnerable, the grace to forgive, and the strength to love unconditionally, creating a ripple effect that touches every part of our lives.

Distorted Expressions

When the Lover archetype gets distorted or stuck in its immature form, it often drifts into daydreaming, fantasy, and romanticism. We start seeking comfort in materialism, piling up shiny objects and toys as if they could somehow manufacture happiness. This immaturity pulls us away from the real struggles and grief of life, luring us into naive optimism. It blinds us to our own pain and the pain of others by denying, minimizing, or glossing over the complex emotions that make us human.

- The Lover's shadow side comes out in ways like **sentimentality**, **nostalgia**, and **romanticism**. These aren't always bad, but when they take over, we end up lost in a world of idealism, charm, and even corny affection. And when the Lover archetype is suppressed, it doesn't just disappear—it often turns into a deep, pervasive depression. This isn't just a passing sadness; it's a hollow emptiness that creeps into every part of life. When we ignore and stifle the Lover, we start losing touch with what once brought us joy—the simple pleasures, the passions that used to ignite our spirit. The world around us keeps moving, but inside, that creative spark, the drive to connect, the capacity to feel deeply—it all gets buried under a weight of unexpressed emotions and unmet needs. Over time, it's like the light inside us dims, making it harder to see the beauty, love, and possibilities that once seemed so clear.

- Not all expressions of the Lover archetype lead to flourishing. When untethered from reality, the

Lover can drift into a distorted form: **The Eternal Optimist**. This version isn't rooted in hope—it's driven by avoidance. The Eternal Optimist refuses to acknowledge pain, loss, or limits, and instead clings to a narrative where everything is always "just fine." It's a mask of positivity worn to shield the heart from grief, and it can become as exhausting as it is isolating.

The Eternal Optimist isn't bad-hearted—they are, in fact, deeply loving. But they have come to believe, often unconsciously, that naming the hard truths will undo them or those around them. They fear that if they stop spinning silver linings, the whole world will unravel. So they smile through heartbreak, speak faith over fracture, and quote inspiration over grief. Their mantra becomes: "Look on the bright side." But this brightness often comes at the cost of intimacy. Because real connection—the kind the Lover longs for— requires truth-telling, even when the truth is painful.

This distortion can be especially common in leaders who want to keep morale high, who have been praised for their positivity, or who grew up in environments where pain wasn't named. The Eternal Optimist may build teams that are energized but shallow, communities that celebrate but don't grieve, and families that smile but silently ache.

The way back is through permission—the courage to allow sorrow, anger, confusion, and longing to coexist with beauty and joy. The Lover doesn't just love what's lovely. In its fullness, it loves what's broken, too. It sees the cracks as sacred, not signs of failure.

When the Eternal Optimist lays down their need to keep everything light, they find that the darkness isn't to be feared it's where the deeper healing and connection begin.

- When the Lover is impaired, it shows up as **the Addicted Lover**. The Addicted Lover is driven by lust, addiction, and hedonism, always chasing new things or ideas but never sticking with them long enough to see any real success. It tries to fill its deep longing for fulfillment and beauty with external distractions, which inevitably lead to obsession or compulsion—a laser focus on a person, substance, or behavior that takes over life. The Lover's natural desire to worship something greater gets hijacked by temporary fixes that never truly satisfy.

- On the flip side, **the Impotent Lover** disconnects from the self and drags us into codependency and enmeshment. In this state, we become obsessed with someone else's well-being, hyper-aware of their feelings and needs while ignoring our own. We lose ourselves in relationships, tying our happiness to how much we can do for others. Instead of expressing our own needs and desires, we give others what we want and need, hoping they'll return the favor—even if they didn't ask for it.

Fulfillment

The Lover finds fulfillment in reciprocal relationships, where it can both give and receive in a balanced way. It discovers what it seeks through passionate devotion to marriage, family, friends, and spiritual communities. In fullness, the Lover embodies emotional depth, sensuality, generosity, gentleness, sensitivity, playfulness, graciousness, and inclusivity. *It understands that heartache and heartbreak are integral to a fulfilling life, recognizing that grief is the mortar that binds the universe together.*

The Lover helps leaders understand and embrace the reality that *"Relationship is essential."* As leaders practice this principle, they're steered away from self-centered desires and toward a love that's expansive and inclusive. It encourages leaders to channel their passion and emotional energy into a greater purpose—whether in relationships, communities, or broader causes. The Lover, under this light, becomes an emblem of unconditional love and selfless devotion, embodying a leadership style that's empathetic, nurturing, and deeply connected to the welfare of others. This shift from self to service transforms the Lover's emotional depth into a powerful tool for building stronger, more compassionate connections.

The Art of Love

Michelangelo's *Pietà* in St. Peter's Basilica is a striking symbol of the Lover archetype in leadership. The sculpture, depicting the Virgin Mary cradling the lifeless body of crucified Jesus, captures the essence of selfless love, compassion, and vulnerability. Mary's tender yet strong embrace reflects a deep connection that transcends personal suffering, focusing entirely on the care and nurturing of another. This is the heart of the Lover archetype in leadership—being willing to carry the emotional burdens of others and leading with a heart full of compassion.

The *Pietà* teaches us that true leadership isn't about power or control; it's about creating a space where others can find comfort and healing. Just as Mary holds Jesus with unwavering love, leaders who embody the Lover archetype do the same for their teams, communities, and loved ones. They understand that leading with love means embracing the full range of human experience—the joy, the pain, the hope, and the heartbreak. The *Pietà* also reminds us that heartbreak is inevitable in both love and leadership. The Lover archetype accepts this truth and finds strength in the vulnerability that comes with deep connection.

In leadership, Michelangelo's *Pietà* serves as a timeless icon of the Lover archetype. It inspires leaders to lead with empathy, to offer themselves in service to others, and to foster environments where love, compassion, and mutual support are the guiding principles. The most profound acts of leadership aren't about grand gestures or displays of authority—they're about quiet, steadfast love that lifts others up, even in the face of deep sorrow.

Ordinary Love

Seeing this sculpture reminded me of one of the purest expressions of the Lover archetype I've ever known: my wife, Heather. Over our thirty years together, life has been anything but predictable marked by both joy and heartbreak. Heather's love doesn't come from grand gestures, but from her steady presence and quiet ability to create space for others. Her leadership isn't about controlling the chaos; it's about cultivating an environment where we're invited to face it together. She influences our family in subtle ways that ripple through everything we do, turning simple moments into something meaningful. Even in the smallest actions, she brings intention and warmth.

She does not call herself a leader, but her quiet influence is at the core of our family's stability. She leads with humility, not force—drawing out the best in each of us, without ever imposing her will. That's what makes her leadership so powerful: it's a steady, grounding presence that gives us a deep sense of place and belonging. Heather's gift is transforming everyday life into something more—a space where we can be fully ourselves. Her leadership, rooted in compassion and generosity, has taught me that leadership isn't about control, but about creating spaces where others can thrive.

Leading with Love

The Lover isn't as much about romantic love or surface emotions; it's about embracing vulnerability, fostering creativity, and building relationships rooted in empathy, compassion, and mutual respect. Leaders who tap into the Lover's energy understand that true influence comes from serving others, not just pursuing their own goals. The Lover shows us that leadership is about putting the needs of others first and guiding them with compassion and understanding.

As leaders, the Lover archetype challenges us to shift from a mindset of self-interest to one of service. It teaches us that real strength lies in our ability to connect deeply with others, to lead with empathy, and to create environments where others can thrive. When we embrace the Lover, we're reminded that life's greatest fulfillment comes not from chasing our own desires, but from dedicating ourselves to something bigger—whether that's in our personal relationships, our communities, or our broader mission in life. By leading with love and compassion, we can build stronger, more connected teams and inspire those around us to grow in their potential.

"

To love another
person is to see the
face of God.

VICTOR HUGO
LES MISÉRABLES

Key Takeaways and Insights:

- **Selflessness and Service:** The Lover archetype teaches that true fulfillment comes from moving beyond self-interest, embracing a life of love, service, and connection.

- **Growth Through Vulnerability:** The Lover's energy emerges in early adulthood, guiding us to connect deeply with others through collaboration, vulnerability, and self-expression.

- **Creative Expression:** The Lover fuels creativity, encouraging us to engage with the world through our senses and build meaningful connections that enrich our lives.

- **Navigating the Shadow Side:** The Lover's energy can be distorted by materialism, addiction, or codependency, leading to unhealthy behaviors that disconnect us from our true selves.

- **Leadership with Empathy:** Embracing the Lover archetype transforms leadership into an act of empathy and compassion, creating environments where everyone can thrive.

Digging Deeper

- How does the Lover archetype show up in your life? Where do you embrace it, and where do you find yourself resisting it?

- Looking back, when did you first notice the Lover archetype emerging in your life? How has its role shifted as you've gotten older?

- How do you define and practice vulnerability in both your personal and professional relationships?

- Think about a time when you felt the tension between loneliness and desire as the Lover archetype. How did you navigate those feelings?

- How do you channel the Lover's energy when you're expressing yourself creatively?

- Reflect on a time when you might have shown the immature or impaired side of the Lover archetype. What led to that, and how did you move past it?

- How does understanding the pitfalls of the "Addicted Lover" or the "Impotent Lover" shape your perspective on maintaining balanced relationships?

- In what ways do you nurture and tap into the Lover's energy in your daily life?

- Reflecting on the idea of fulfillment, how do you see grief as the "mortar that binds the universe together?"

- How will a deeper understanding of the Lover archetype change your approach to relationships, creativity, and self-expression going forward?

The King/Queen

"Control is an illusion."

When it comes to leadership, the King/Queen archetype guides leaders to cast the vision, set the course, and lay the foundations of a thriving kingdom with a presence that creates security, defines boundaries, allocates resources, and fosters a culture of growth.

This archetype is the shield against chaos, the voice of hope in times of change, and the guiding hand during crises, steering the kingdom toward stability, order, and vitality. It bears the weight of tough decisions, cultivating individuals and organizations while embracing the ever-present tension between life and death. The King/Queen archetype enables evolution, growth, and innovation while simultaneously pruning and eliminating what's languishing, so the whole can thrive.

Abraham Lincoln's leadership during the Civil War is a prime example of the King/Queen archetype in action. He didn't just hold power; he shouldered the responsibility of guiding a divided nation through its darkest hour. Lincoln knew he had to balance justice with mercy, making tough, often unpopular decisions, all while staying grounded in humility and moral clarity.

Faced with the challenge of preserving the Union and addressing slavery, Lincoln looked beyond the immediate crisis to a vision of a united, free nation. His decisions, like the Emancipation Proclamation and the Gettysburg Address, weren't just about keeping the Union intact—they were about redefining what it stood for. Even when the path was uncertain, Lincoln's commitment to the greater good never wavered.

Lincoln's legacy as a leader shows the King archetype at its best. He understood that real power isn't about dominance; it's about guiding others toward a shared vision, even in the face of adversity. His ability to make tough, principled decisions with humility and a focus on service left an indelible mark on the nation, proving that true leadership is about serving something bigger than yourself.

Royal Secret: Humility Wears the Crown

Indra Nooyi's time as CEO of PepsiCo is a textbook example of the King/Queen archetype in action. She didn't just run a company; she led with a vision that tied financial success directly to social responsibility. Her concept of "Performance with Purpose" wasn't just about doing good—it was about ensuring PepsiCo could thrive in the long run. Nooyi understood that balancing short-term gains with long-term goals was key, especially in tough times. She knew that focusing on sustainability—both environmental and human—wasn't just the right thing to do, it was smart business.

Nooyi wasn't afraid to make tough calls, like shifting PepsiCo toward healthier products, even when it wasn't the most popular move at the time. She redefined the boundaries of what PepsiCo could be. Her push for environmental sustainability wasn't just about saving the planet—it was about cutting costs and staying relevant in a world that's increasingly focused on being green. Nooyi also prioritized the well-being of her team, understanding that happy, healthy employees are the backbone of a successful company. She made sure PepsiCo was a place where people wanted to work, not just a place they had to work.

Nooyi believed that to really succeed globally, you've got to think locally. Nooyi didn't lead from behind a desk—she spent time in places like China, getting to know the culture and understanding what people there really needed. This approach allowed her to lead with empathy and insight, making sure PepsiCo's global strategies weren't just effective but also culturally on point. Throughout her leadership, Nooyi showed the patience, vision, and nuanced understanding that define a true King/Queen.

Phase

The qualities of the King/Queen start to reveal themselves in the late thirties or early forties and become more active throughout the forties and into the late fifties. As leaders begin to sense that more of life lies behind them than ahead, the King/Queen evokes a sense of legacy. They start asking, *"What can I grow beyond myself?"* and *"What will I leave behind?"* It's in this season that leaders must face the reality that life is short, and they won't accomplish everything they dream of. It's also when we begin to appreciate that every choice is both a gain and a loss.

Posture

The King/Queen lets leaders see the paradoxical nature of life, enabling them to know that truth is objective, yet it can only be subjectively encountered. Unlike the Warrior and Lover, whose vision is often a dream, the King/Queen sees how things could be and understands how they likely won't be. It sharpens a leader's awareness that what got them here won't get them where they want to be and helps them sense that everything will be something more—and something less—than what it could be.

Relationally, the King/Queen helps leaders soothe the drives of the Warrior and Lover, pushing them to overcome personal insecurities so the greater good is served. It shifts the focus to serving the kingdom, ensuring that the whole can flourish, which in turn frees the individual contributors to become healthier, wiser, freer, and more autonomous. The whole, not the individual, is the top priority. The King/Queen archetype empowers leaders to seek council, helping them recognize they don't have all the answers—and maybe not even the right questions.

Psychologically, the King/Queen helps leaders keep heart as they face unavoidable ambivalence and two-choice dilemmas. It allows us to tolerate competing desires so we can make hard choices. It makes us increasingly aware that "things fade" and "alternatives exclude."[10] Together, these phrases reveal the fragile dance between possibility and necessity at the heart of human experience.

It helps us realize how short our time here is and come to terms with the fact that every choice carries the shadow of loss. From deep within, questions bubble up like:

- *What is my real purpose?*

- *What is my true significance?*

- *What does it all mean?*

- *How will I be remembered?*

- *What will be my legacy?*

Spiritually, the King/Queen archetype allows us to enter life's dualities, helping leaders relate to themselves, others, and GOD with a both/and mindset. This archetype sits at the crossroads of heaven and earth and mediates opposing but equally powerful forces like:

- Justice/Mercy

- Life/Death

- Good/Evil

- Order/Chaos

- Innocence/Experience

Practice

For leaders, the King/Queen creates a strong center through infrastructure, guidelines, processes, and standards of performance, compensation, and reward. They accept the responsibility to hire, fire, promote, demote, and reassign team members. The King/Queen archetype is motivated by the long play. It moves us toward patience, delayed gratification, surrender, acceptance, and cultivation. The King/Queen helps us see where the edges of things need to be and draws the lines accordingly. When we're using the skills of the King/Queen, "Yes" and "No" become clearer, and we're more able to set boundaries. We grow willing to say "No" to people, places, and things that drain our life and energy so we can say "Yes!" to what aligns with our mission and empowers the kingdom.

The King/Queen becomes adept at acceptance, helping us realize and appreciate the necessity of loss as a fundamental part of life. It empowers us to lean into acceptance and provides us the capacity for necessary endings. The King/Queen understands that good/bad and right/wrong are limited categories, and that situational context matters—one size doesn't fit all. It helps us develop a nuanced understanding of human nature with a keen sense of timing and allows us to accept that life has more shades of gray than many are comfortable with.

Power

Optimistically realistic, the King/Queen is driven by a vision of how things could be yet grounded in the acceptance and grief of what they'll never be. It's a posture of both invitation and exclusion. "Come join the noble mission, live in the abundance of the kingdom, AND the standard for continued participation is _____." As a source of inspiration and creativity, the King/Queen calls others to more and engages the world with hope, steadfastness, and clarity. It lets leaders use their experience, expertise, and perspective to set the course, inspire participation, and maintain accountability. In humility, the King/Queen enables leaders to shoulder the loneliness of their position for the blessing of others.

Distorted Expressions

The distorted Kings/Queen archetypes leave leaders deeply insecure, often without realizing it. They trap us in a scarcity mindset, tempting us to destroy anything that feels like a threat to our security. Leaders like this end up ruling a fragile kingdom,

"

The King/Queen becomes adept at *acceptance*, helping us realize and appreciate the *necessity of loss* as a *fundamental part of life.*

where a shadow narcissism starts to creep in. They surround themselves with people who "need" them, but as they let others take advantage, they become paranoid, reclusive, and isolated. With no real boundaries, they start exploiting others—using them as pawns, abusing them, or tossing them under the bus to get ahead.

Marie Antoinette is often associated with this kind of detached and irresponsible Queen archetype. Even though the phrase "Let them eat cake" might be apocryphal, it sums up her perceived indifference to the suffering of her people. Her lavish lifestyle and lack of empathy for the struggles of the lower classes only fueled the anger that led to the French Revolution. Marie Antoinette's life serves as a cautionary tale— a Queen who failed to grasp the needs of her people and the responsibilities of her position, leading to tragic consequences.

- One way the underdeveloped King/Queen shows up is as **the King/Queen Baby**. This is the person who craves attention and constant reassurance. They want to take as much as they can and they give little to nothing in return. This immature King/Queen demands instant gratification, expecting the world to revolve around them. And when it doesn't, well, there's hell to pay.

- Then there's **the Tyrant**—a different, but equally impaired, version of the King/Queen archetype. This leader is all about accumulating power and staying on top, even if it means standing alone. The Tyrant bullies others into serving them, rather than serving the kingdom. Think Emperor Nero, the classic Tyrant. His reign was marked by self-indulgence, cruelty, and paranoia. Nero eliminated anyone he perceived as threat, often through brutal means, causing widespread suffering and instability. His leadership shows us the dark side of the King/Queen archetype—a ruler driven by fear and self-interest rather than justice and compassion.

- **The "Mr. Nice Guy/Ms. Nice Gal"** archetype—is another destructive but often overlooked impaired expression of the impaired King/Queen. This posture isn't just about being nice; it's about a practiced weakness where motivation, initiative, and boundaries are in short supply. When we fall into this posture, we tend to martyr ourselves, giving more than is good for us and more than others can handle.

  The problem is, without solid boundaries, we start feeling resentful when others don't meet our unspoken expectations. And when we finally do say something or act, it's usually passive-aggressive. The Nice Guy/Gal avoids making decisions, letting others take the lead, and in doing so, opens the door for exploitation. Take Neville Chamberlain, the British Prime Minister before World War II. He's often seen as the ultimate "Mr. Nice Guy" in his dealings with Hitler. Chamberlain's policy of appeasement, especially the signing of the Munich Agreement in 1938, was meant to keep the peace at any cost. But this approach lacked the necessary boundaries and firmness, allowing Hitler to take advantage of his generosity. What started as well-intentioned, even noble, ended up looking weak and contributed to a conflict that could've been avoided.

Fulfillment

In its fullest expression, the King/Queen provides order and opportunities that bless the lives of others through participation in the vision and structures the King/Queen has created. This archetype helps us become masters of collaborative synergy as we learn to inspire, align, direct, equip, and empower others. The fullness of the King/Queen seeks to "grow the pie" because they understand that the larger whole creates more resources and opportunities. The fulfilled King/Queen understands that power and influence increases the more they share it with others. The King/Queen finds their ultimate fulfillment and legacy in service to the kingdom and focuses primarily on the growth and well-being of others and the communities they guide. They become a servant-leader.

As leaders evolve toward being a servant-leader, they begin to face the profound truth that "Control is an illusion." This realization serves as a humbling force, reminding leaders that their true greatness lies not in personal glory or dominion but in their ability to serve and uplift the Kingdom. The King/Queen, when guided by this understanding, evolves from a figure of mere authority to a leadership style that prioritizes collective well-being over personal security, reinforcing the true essence of a servant-leader. In this light, the King/Queen becomes not just a leader, but a guardian of their community's values and a catalyst for collective growth.

"

The problem is, without solid boundaries, we start feeling *resentful* when others don't meet our *unspoken expectations.*

It's Not About You

Leadership goes way beyond just having a title or position—it's about serving something bigger than ourselves. The King/Queen archetype shows us that leadership isn't about seeking personal glory or clinging to power; it's about using that authority, responsibility, and influence to create a thriving, sustainable environment for others. Whether it's Abraham Lincoln leading a nation through its darkest days or Indra Nooyi guiding a global company with a focus on long-term purpose, the heart of the King/Queen is found in humility, vision, and stewardship.

The journey of a leader who embodies the King/Queen archetype is all about growth and reflection. It's about understanding that every decision we make has a ripple effect, and that with every choice comes both gain and loss. It's about learning to hold justice with mercy, authority with empathy, and vision with reality. When we shift our focus from ourselves to the well-being of those we lead, we unlock a deeper, more lasting influence— one that goes beyond the immediate and leaves a legacy of positive impact.

In the end, the King/Queen archetype challenges us to move from being mere rulers to becoming guardians of our communities, organizations, and the world. By embracing humility and realizing that we're not as important as the mission we serve, we become leaders who don't just hold power, but who lift others up, inspire growth, and leave behind a legacy of collective well-being. True fulfillment comes not from personal accolades, but from seeing those we've led flourish.

"

If you want to lift yourself up, lift up someone else.

BOOKER T. WASHINGTON

Key Takeaways and Insights:

- **Legacy Over Ambition:** The King/Queen archetype shifts leaders from focusing on personal ambition to thinking about what they'll leave behind. It's about building something that lasts beyond you.

- **Power with Humility:** True leadership in the King/Queen mode balances power with humility. It's not about dominating; it's about using your authority, responsibility, and influence to serve the greater good.

- **Navigating Life's Contradictions:** The King/Queen helps you see and accept life's dualities—like justice and mercy, order and chaos. It's about understanding that truth is complex and decisions aren't always black and white.

- **Watch Out for Immaturity:** Immature expressions of the King/Queen, like being a Tyrant or a Nice Guy/Gal, can seriously mess up your leadership. Recognizing these tendencies and keeping them in check is crucial.

- **Serve to Grow:** The ultimate King/Queen leads by serving others. Focusing on the growth and well-being of your community, rather than personal control or recognition, creates lasting impact and a true legacy.

Digging Deeper

- How does the King/Queen archetype resonate with the deepest longings of your heart? How can you use this to guide your leadership journey?

- How does the King/Queen's focus on the "greater good" challenge our individualistic perspectives?

- The King/Queen understands that truth is objective but can only be subjectively encountered. How does this statement reflect in your understanding of leadership?

- How can organizations incorporate the principles of infrastructure, guidelines, and processes emphasized by the King/Queen for more effective leadership?

- How does the King/Queen archetype address the need for acceptance and understanding the limitations and nuances of life?

- What personal qualities do you think are essential for someone to truly embody the King or Queen archetype in their leadership?

- In what ways can you cultivate a legacy that outlasts your tenure as a leader? Think about the structures, relationships, or values you're building now—how will they continue to impact your organization or community after you've moved on?

- How does your current leadership style reflect the long-term vision of the King/Queen archetype? Are you focused on immediate gains or on sustainable, long-term growth?

- In what ways might the immature expressions of the King/Queen distort your leadership? Where have you been on the receiving end of distorted forms of The King/Queen leadership?

- What barriers might be preventing you from embracing the true King/Queen within, and how can you confront and move beyond these barriers?

The Sage

"Everything is as it's intended."

With mental calmness, composure, and evenness of temper, the Sage archetype allows for equanimity in leadership. In stark contrast to other archetypes, the Sage seems paradoxical, helping leaders confront life's harshest realities with nuanced understanding.

It operates from a place of deep intuition, acting as the Great Teacher within us, fueling intellectual curiosity and the quest for sacred and hidden knowledge. The Sage leads us to value both knowledge and ignorance; experience and innocence; tradition and novelty.

Characters like Yoda from *Star Wars*, Gandalf from *The Lord of the Rings*, Dumbledore from *Harry Potter*, Morpheus from *The Matrix*, and Professor X from *X-Men* are classic examples of the Sage archetype in popular culture. These leaders don't just hold power—they guide others through life's toughest challenges with deep wisdom and insight. Yoda taps into the mysteries of the Force, Gandalf sees beyond immediate battles to the bigger picture, Dumbledore navigates moral complexities, Morpheus challenges us to question our reality, and Professor X envisions a world where everyone can coexist peacefully. What ties them all together is their ability to lead through understanding, reflection, and a deep sense of purpose. They don't just tell others what to do—they help them discover their own strength and potential, all while navigating the deeper truths that shape their worlds.

In real life Socrates, Gandhi, Confucius, Mandela, and Leonardo da Vinci all capture what it means to be a Sage. Socrates led his students on a journey of self-discovery, always stressing that real wisdom starts with admitting what you don't know. Gandhi showed that true power isn't about force—it's about moral authority, using nonviolence to lead India to independence. Confucius focused on wisdom and virtue, guiding others toward harmony through self-reflection. Mandela, after years in prison, came out committed to reconciliation, leading South Africa through its hardest moments with patience and moral clarity. Then there's Leonardo da Vinci, whose insatiable curiosity and drive to connect the dots in everything made him the ultimate Renaissance man. These leaders guided the illumination of others with deep integration and wisdom.

Phase

The Sage archetype begins to emerge in our late forties and fifties, gaining momentum through the sixties and seventies, and often continues beyond. In this season, leaders start to grasp that time is both fleeting and eternal. The Sage guides leaders from structure to openness, from knowing to curiosity, from confidence to humility, and from certainty to wonder. *It's a time when the Sage enables leaders to confront their own insignificance and recognize the importance of stepping aside to let others ascend. They begin to wonder, "How can I maintain my significance while I become increasingly irrelevant?"*

Posture

The Sage archetype invites leaders to dig into the deeper, often hidden layers of life and leadership. Through the posture of the Sage, leaders understand that leadership is not about grasping more power or chasing success; it's about understanding

66

It's a time when the Sage enables leaders to *confront their own insignificance* and recognize the importance of *stepping aside* to let others *ascend*.

the subtleties of human experience—both within us, in our relationships with others, and in the systems we navigate. The Sage urges leaders to step back from the frantic pace of proving, conquering, and winning, to encourage a more authentic and reflective approach to life.

Relationally, the Sage encourages leaders to engage authentically without the need to prove, conquer, or win. Quick to listen and slow to speak, this archetype fosters curiosity, presence, and attunement to others. *It gives leaders the wisdom to accept the inherent loneliness that accompanies leadership roles or the natural process of aging.*

Psychologically, the Sage archetype encourages healthy introspection and reflection, allowing leaders to trust the deep process of life, death, and renewal. It prompts leaders to ponder profound questions like *"What is truly meaningful?"* and *"How can I be of service?"* This archetype allows leaders to integrate the gifts and limit the impairments of the Warrior, Lover, and King/Queen archetypes.

Spiritually, the Sage archetype invites us to transcend dualistic concepts and theological barriers, leading us toward the unfathomable depths of wisdom beyond comprehension. *It invites us into the realm of mystery and eternity, where Truth can only be encountered, never named.* Embracing meditation, prayer, contemplation, and devotion, it acts as a mediator between the seen and unseen aspects of life.

Practice

The Sage archetype is all about having an informed perspective. It helps us comprehend and integrate wisdom, accumulated knowledge, and experience. It helps leaders learn from the past and dream of a new future. It narrows and expands their influence, authority, and responsibilities through curiosity, wonder, and the surrender of power. It helps us notice, accept, and acknowledge our limitations.

Leaders adept in the Sage archetype know how and when to wait to let things play themselves out because they understand that often the best outcomes can't be predicted or manufactured—they just have to be. In this way, the Sage archetype lets leaders embrace a perspective that says, *"We'll see," Maybe,"* and *"What if?"*

The Sage allows leaders to accumulate wisdom through diligent application of knowledge and experiential learning grounded in discernment of deeper wisdom. It helps leaders understand the lessons of the past and envision the possibilities of the future. Rather than wielding strength as its primary energy, the Sage archetype gives leaders secret knowledge of how the world operates, empowering them to manipulate systems to achieve desired outcomes. *The Sage helps leaders work beyond the edges of convention, enable innovation, and bend the rules in their favor.*

Power

By embracing paradox and trusting mystery, the Sage archetype becomes a wellspring of inspiration, dreams, humor, and invitation. It allows leaders to patiently use their experience and wisdom to help followers trust the process of becoming. This is the binding energy of the other three archetypes and at its best integrates the energies of the Warrior, Lover, and King/Queen so that leaders can know the appropriate time to bring what is needed to the conversation, situation, or context, without the need to be recognized in the outcomes. When connected to the Warrior, the Sage archetype allows the Warrior to break the right rules at the right time. When combined with the Lover, it helps leaders mentor, advise, and coach. When integrated into the King/Queen, the Sage archetype fuels wisdom, innovation, and vision.

Distorted Expressions

The Sage archetype also has its shadow side which can lead us astray. Instead of guiding us toward wisdom and insight, the Sage can turn leaders into a **Daydreamer**, a **Manipulator**, an **Observer**, a **"Know-It-All,"** or a **Nostalgic**. *These impaired versions of the Sage can cause a lot of damage, both to the individual and to those around them.*

- **The Daydreamer** is always looking for shortcuts and the easy way out, but never really committing to excellence. This mindset breeds laziness and jealousy, fueling fantasies of effortless success. Walter Mitty from *The Secret Life of Walter Mitty* is a classic example of this. He's constantly lost in grand fantasies and adventures, but when it comes to real life, he struggles to act—until he's finally pushed to confront his daydreams head-on.

- Another version of the Sage that goes off course is **the Manipulator**—the huckster or conman.

66

These impaired versions of the Sage can cause a lot of damage, both to the *individual* and to *those around them.*

This shadow Sage dangles the promise of secret knowledge just out of reach, never fully sharing what they know. Instead, they withhold key information to feed their pride and line their pockets. These manipulators pretend to be experts who've got the key to life's secrets. We see them everywhere—from Wall Street to Washington, Madison Avenue to First Church USA. Bernie Madoff is a prime example. He sold himself as a financial genius, promising exclusive insights, and high returns, but was actually running the biggest Ponzi scheme in history. His manipulation wasn't just about money; it was about exploiting the trust of his investors to feed his own ego and wealth.

- Then there's **the Observer**—a Sage so caught up in analysis that they're paralyzed by it. This type stays detached, wrapped in a self-made maze of "what ifs" and endless pros and cons. They become a spectator in life rather than a participant. Hamlet, from Shakespeare's play, is the perfect example. He's trapped in indecision, endlessly analyzing every possible outcome, which ultimately leads to his downfall. His overthinking and fear of making the wrong move turn him into an Observer, keeping him stuck in place.

- This Observer can also morph into **the "Know-it-All,"** rigid in their thinking and convinced they've got all the answers. But this attitude often pushes others away, creating a false sense of security in their knowledge while alienating those around them. The Know-it-All becomes critical, judgmental, and arrogant, using their supposed wisdom as a shield against the mysteries of life. The character Sheldon Cooper (from *The Big Bang Theory*) is a brilliant physicist but often comes across as a Know-it-All due to his rigid thinking and lack of social awareness. His arrogance and belief that he has all the answers often alienate his friends and colleagues.

- Finally, there's **the Nostalgic Sage**, who's entranced by a longing for "the good old days." This version of the Sage is stuck in a past that never really was as perfect as they remember. They're blinded by nostalgia, which keeps them from seeing the present clearly or imagining a better future. Uncle Rico from *Napoleon Dynamite* is a great example. He's obsessed with his high school football days, convinced his life would've been perfect if only he could go back. His nostalgia traps him in the past, stopping him from moving forward or making the most of his current life, demanding that others enter the fantasy he tries to perpetuate.

Fulfillment

In its fullest expression, the Sage is the "alchemist of life" who helps leaders transform disappointment, heartbreak, and setbacks into opportunities for learning, growth, and innovation. Rather than hoarding wisdom, the Sage inspires others, and shares knowledge generously, without ego and need for recognition.

The Sage equips leaders to stay calm in crisis and rooted in trustworthy process (not outcomes) so that leaders can be a source of simple clarity, stable guidance, and integrative wisdom.

Within this context, the Sage invites us to accept our own short-lived existence. It helps leaders understand, accept, and embrace the impermanence of all things—especially themselves. In doing so leaders come to the wisdom that *"Everything is as it's intended."*

Embracing this nurtures a profound wisdom and adaptability in leaders, traits intrinsic to the Sage's essence. This acceptance enriches the Sage's perspective, allowing for a more nuanced understanding of leadership's fluid dynamics. The Sage's unflinching confrontation with mortality serves as a critical reminder of the urgency and significance of purpose-oriented leadership. This awareness, implores leaders to prioritize what is beautiful, true, and good, fostering a leadership style that's not only effective but also practical and meaningful. By integrating these realities, the Sage archetype not only aids in navigating the complexities of leadership but also in crafting a path that resonates with depth, authenticity, and enduring impact.

"

All I know is that I know nothing.

SOCRATES

Key Takeaways and Insights:

- **Embrace Paradox and Humility:** The Sage archetype shows us that real wisdom comes from embracing the messiness of life—valuing both what we know and what we don't. It's about leading with humility, acknowledging limitations, not trying to have all the answers, but helping others find their way.

- **Navigate Life's Complexities:** The Sage helps us face life's toughest moments with calmness, perspective, and curiosity. It's about shifting from needing certainty to being open to the unknown, making leadership less about control and more about exploration and possibility.

- **Turn Challenges into Growth:** At its best, the Sage turns life's setbacks into steppingstones for growth. It's about seeing every challenge, big or small, as a chance to learn, integrate, and synthesize, not just for yourself but for those you lead.

- **Watch Out for the Sage's Dark Side:** The Sage can go off course, leading to inaction, manipulation, or getting stuck in the past. It's a reminder to stay grounded in wisdom, keep learning, and avoid falling into the traps of daydreaming, deceit, or nostalgia.

- **Accept Mortality and Uncertainty:** The Sage pushes us to confront the hard truths—we're not in control, and we're not here forever. By embracing these realities, we can discern and focus on what really matters, leading with purpose and making a lasting impact where it counts.

Digging Deeper

- Who in your life embodies the Sage archetype? What lessons have you learned from them?

- How does the idea that the Sage values both "knowledge and ignorance" resonate with your understanding of wisdom?

- How can modern leaders benefit from transitioning from "structure to openness" and "certainty to wonder?"

- Reflect on a time when you prioritized listening over speaking. How did it influence the outcome of the situation?

- In what ways can transcending "dualistic concepts and theological barriers" lead to a richer spiritual understanding?

- How can adopting a "We'll see" or "What if?" perspective be beneficial in leadership?

- Can you recall a situation where experiential learning or application of knowledge resulted in unexpected wisdom?

- Have you ever encountered a leader who embodied the "Manipulator, "Observer," or "Nostalgic" expressions of the Sage? How did it impact their leadership?

- Can you identify moments when you've embodied any of the immature or impaired versions of the Sage, such as the Daydreamer, Manipulator, Observer, Know-It-All, or Nostalgic? How did these moments affect your decision-making or relationships?

- Reflect on a significant setback or disappointment in your life. How did you, or how might you, transform that experience into an opportunity for growth, learning, or innovation, as the Sage does?

Putting It
Into Practice

The Warrior, Lover, King/Queen, and Sage aren't just abstract ideas—they represent a unique way of knowing, being, doing, and seeing that guides us toward becoming more conscious leaders, living lives filled with meaning. Together, these archetypes form an Inner Council of Wisdom, a toolkit for navigating the complexities of leadership and life with greater clarity, connection, and confidence.

As we practice leadership, we often find ourselves embodying different aspects of these archetypes. The Warrior's quest for identity and courage, the Lover's deep dive into emotions and relationships, the King/Queen's call to lead with wisdom and authority, and the Sage's pursuit of reflection and shared wisdom—all these stages give us vital wisdom. While we might naturally lean more toward one or two archetypes, recognizing and integrating all four into our consciousness allows us to understand ourselves and others more deeply. This understanding helps us become more courageous, compassionate, effective, and influential leaders, equipped to adapt our approach to whatever challenges life throws our way.

True transformation—whether in leadership or life—isn't merely a process of executing a plan; it's about engaging with the deeper, unseen forces that shape who we are and what we become. By drawing on the wisdom of symbols, myths, and archetypes, we access a map that guides us toward becoming leaders who don't just achieve tasks—they inspire others, initiate meaningful change, and leave an enduring legacy.

A full-hearted leader understands that mastering these dynamics isn't the goal; practicing them is. This framework is about blending these diverse aspects of leadership into our daily lives, enhancing our self-awareness, adaptability, and influence. By embracing this evolving wisdom, we can navigate life with integrated courage, passion, authority, and insight, fostering a more compassionate, adaptable, and resilient approach to both life and leadership.

By viewing challenges through the lens of these archetypes, you can uncover fresh perspectives and approaches for navigating your current decisions and obstacles.

The following exercise is designed to help you deepen your awareness of each archetype's wisdom and to use that insight in practical ways. Use this worksheet to gain clarity and broaden your perspective on a recent leadership challenge.

- **Step 1:** Identify a current issue where you feel blocked or burdened—one that requires courage, compassion, confidence, or clarity you're struggling to find. What feels heavy or unresolved?

- **Step 2:** Engage each archetype's perspective by answering these questions:

    Definition – What story or narrative does each archetype offer about this situation? How would each interpret the essence of the challenge?

    Perception – How does this archetype perceive and emotionally respond to the issue? What thoughts or feelings are central to its view?

    Response – What course of action does each archetype suggest?

- **Step 3:** Reflect on the insights you've gathered.

  - How might these perspectives reshape, expand, or refine your approach to this issue?

  - How might these reflections influence your broader approach to leadership?

ISSUE:			
ARCHETYPE	PERCEPTION	DEFINITION	RESPONSE
Warrior			
Lover			
King/Queen			
Sage			

Digging Deeper

- How does blending the Warrior, Lover, King/Queen, and Sage energies create a well-rounded leader?

- Which of these four archetypes speaks to you the most? What about it stirs your heart and sparks your curiosity?

- Try drawing each archetype—really get into the details. What do these drawings reveal about your connection to each one?

- Everyone has a unique mix of these archetypal energies. How could someone harness the strengths of all four at once?

- How does understanding these archetypes boost your decision-making as a leader?

- Each archetype offers its own set of tools. Can you think of a situation where using multiple archetypes at once might be helpful?

- How can someone smoothly shift from one archetype to another, especially when life throws a curveball?

- How do these archetypes influence dynamics among people at work? Those at home? Could knowing another person's dominant archetype improve collaboration?

- Archetypes are powerful sources of energy. How might you tap into or channel these energies during personal or professional challenges?

- How do these archetypes help nurture not just leadership but also personal relationships and self-growth?

Acknowledgments

This book wouldn't exist without the incredible people who supported, challenged, and inspired me along the way.

First, to all the members of Council Leadership— thank you for letting me work out this material with you. Your feedback, encouragement, and willingness to engage with these ideas gave me the clarity and insight needed to better understand this framework and its potential applications.

To the Council Leadership team—especially Scott Hearon, Dane Anthony, Rachel Rochefort, and Brett Williams—thank you for your patience and invaluable feedback. A special thank you to Dane, who served as a thought partner in the early stages of developing these ideas. Your wisdom and perspective were key to bringing this vision to life.

And to the incredible team at Circa Brand Agency— Tori Thomas, Sonya Watson, Chloe Thompson, and Megan Ervin—thank you for making this book something as beautiful as I imagined. Your creativity and expertise turned my vision into something truly extraordinary.

Appendix A: Examples of Archetypes

 *Warrior*

"Courage is not having the strength to go on; it is going on when you don't have the strength."—Theodore Roosevelt

Alexander the Great: A Macedonian king with a drive for conquest, Alexander took on the known world in the 4th century BCE. His strategic brilliance and leadership made him a legendary warrior who carved out an empire that stretched across continents.

Joan of Arc: Known as the "Maid of Orleans," Joan led French forces during the Hundred Years' War. Her unshakable faith and courage inspired her troops, making her a symbol of the Warrior spirit.

Genghis Khan: As the founder of the Mongol Empire, Genghis Khan was a force to be reckoned with. His strategic genius and relentless ambition allowed him to build one of history's largest empires, defining what it means to be a Warrior.

Leonidas I (Historical): King Leonidas of Sparta famously led 300 Spartans at the Battle of Thermopylae. His bravery and sacrifice against overwhelming odds have made his name synonymous with the Warrior archetype.

Nelson Mandela: While not a warrior in the traditional sense, Mandela fought a different kind of battle—against apartheid. His resilience and determination in the face of immense adversity embody the Warrior spirit.

Aragorn (*The Lord of the Rings*): Aragorn, the skilled ranger and rightful king, steps into his role as a leader in the fight against Sauron. He embodies the Warrior's honor, bravery, and selflessness.

Maximus Decimus Meridius (*Gladiator*): A Roman general turned gladiator; Maximus seeks justice against a corrupt emperor. His strength, determination, and resilience make him a classic Warrior figure.

Wonder Woman: Wonder Woman embodies the Warrior Archetype through her strength, courage, and unwavering commitment to justice, always fighting to protect the vulnerable and uphold peace. She balances power with compassion, using her disciplined skills and moral integrity to serve as a force for good in a complex world.

Buffy Summers (*Buffy the Vampire Slayer*): Buffy blends physical combat skills with emotional strength as she battles supernatural forces. She's a modern Warrior who fights with both her heart and her fists.

John Wick: A retired hitman seeking vengeance, John Wick is relentless and resourceful. His single-minded determination and lethal skill set make him the ultimate modern Warrior.

Katniss Everdeen (*The Hunger Games*): A skilled archer and survivor, Katniss becomes the face of rebellion against a dystopian regime. Her courage and spirit of defiance are pure Warrior.

Lover

"The best way to find yourself is to lose yourself in the service of others." –Mahatma Gandhi

Sojourner Truth: Born into slavery, Sojourner became a leading voice for abolition and women's rights. Her love for her children, especially her fight to win back her son, reflects the deep compassion and dedication of the Lover archetype.

Mother Teresa: Known worldwide for her boundless compassion, Mother Teresa devoted her life to the sick and poor. Her selflessness and care for others are the epitome of the Lover archetype.

Mahatma Gandhi: Gandhi's commitment to nonviolence and his love for humanity led him to fight for India's independence. His life is a powerful example of the Lover's deep empathy and devotion.

Penelope (Homer's *Odyssey*): While Odysseus is away, Penelope's unwavering love and faithfulness keep her steadfast, showcasing the Lover's enduring commitment and strength.

Samwise Gamgee (*The Lord of the Rings*): Sam's loyalty and dedication to Frodo are the essence of the Lover archetype. His friendship and selfless support are what keep the journey alive.

Frida Kahlo: The artist Frida Kahlo personifies the Lover Archetype, expressing profound emotion, sensuality, and a deep exploration of her inner life through her art, allowing her vulnerability and passion to resonate universally.

Jack Dawson (*Titanic*): Jack's passionate devotion to Rose, seeing beauty in every moment, and ultimately sacrificing himself, captures the heart of the Lover archetype.

Noah Calhoun (*The Notebook*): Noah's unwavering love for Allie, especially in the face of her Alzheimer's, embodies the Lover's enduring commitment and devotion.

Maya Angelou: With her poetry and prose, Angelou embodied the Lover/Mother Archetype by nurturing readers' spirits and creating a powerful sense of connection, resilience, and healing, especially for those marginalized or oppressed.

Orpheus (Greek mythology): Orpheus's deep love for Eurydice drives him to the underworld to bring her back, making him a timeless example of the Lover's power.

Marmee March (from *Little Women*): Marmee is a compassionate and wise mother who nurtures her daughters through adversity and encourages them to grow into their authentic selves. She embodies the Lover/Mother Archetype by providing her children with both moral guidance and unconditional love.

Westley (*The Princess Bride*): Westley's dedication to Buttercup, summarized in "As you wish," showcases the Lover's unwavering love and commitment.

Joyce Byers (*Stranger Things*): A determined mother who goes to great lengths to find her missing son, Joyce's love and commitment highlight the Lover's deep emotional connection.

 *King/Queen*

"Nearly all men can stand adversity, but if you want to test a man's character, give him power." –Abraham Lincoln

King Leonidas I: Led 300 Spartans against a massive Persian army at Thermopylae, showcasing a King's fearless courage and unyielding resolve in the face of impossible odds.

King David (Biblical): United Israel and established Jerusalem as its capital. His visionary leadership and devotion to God make him a profound representation of the King archetype.

Aslan (*The Chronicles of Narnia*): The wise and just lion who created and protected Narnia, embodying a King's benevolent authority and sacrificial love.

Queen Catherine the Great: Expanded Russia's borders and nurtured the arts, illustrating the Queen archetype through her transformative power and cultural impact.

King George VI: Unexpectedly called to the throne, George VI led Britain through World War II with quiet strength and perseverance, demonstrating the King's resilience in adversity.

Aragorn (*The Lord of the Rings*): From a ranger to the rightful King of Gondor, Aragorn's journey reflects the King's call to embrace destiny, leading with wisdom and valor.

King T'Challa (*Black Panther*): As the Black Panther and King of Wakanda, T'Challa's blend of strength, justice, and humility captures the essence of a leader who serves his people with honor.

Simba (*The Lion King*): From a hesitant cub to a responsible leader, Simba's story is a classic King's journey of overcoming self-doubt and stepping into his role with courage.

Queen Esther (Biblical): Risked her life to save her people, exemplifying a Queen's courage, wisdom, and ability to navigate complex political terrain for the sake of others.

King Solomon (Biblical): Known for his unparalleled wisdom and discernment, Solomon represents a King's gift of judgment and the capacity to bring peace through understanding.

Eleanor Roosevelt: As First Lady and a champion for human rights, Eleanor's influence and commitment to justice reflect the Queen archetype's nurturing strength and societal impact.

Angela Merkel: Guided Germany through economic and political turbulence, embodying the Queen's qualities of calm, pragmatic leadership and fostering stability during crisis.

Abraham Lincoln: Steered the United States through the Civil War and the abolition of slavery, demonstrating a King's integrity, vision, and unshakable moral courage.

Golda Meir: The fourth Prime Minister of Israel, Meir's steadfast leadership during the Yom Kippur War epitomizes the Queen's resilience and fierce protectiveness.

Ronald Reagan: Known for his charismatic leadership during the Cold War and optimistic vision for America, Reagan exemplifies the King's ability to inspire and guide a nation through turbulent times.

Sage

"The fool doth think he is wise, but the wise man knows himself to be a fool."—William Shakespeare (As You Like It)

Socrates: Known for his pursuit of wisdom and the Socratic method, Socrates exemplifies the Sage archetype through his dedication to understanding and guiding others in their own quests for knowledge.

Confucius: A Chinese philosopher whose teachings on ethics and education have shaped cultures for centuries, Confucius embodies the Sage's role as a teacher and guide.

Gandalf (*The Lord of the Rings*): Gandalf's deep wisdom and guidance throughout Middle-earth make him a classic Sage, always steering others toward the right path with insight and foresight.

Yoda (*Star Wars*): Yoda, the wise Jedi Master, imparts knowledge and guidance to the younger generation, perfectly capturing the Sage's role in teaching and mentoring.

Merlin (Arthurian Legends): Merlin, the legendary advisor to King Arthur, uses his wisdom and magical abilities to guide and protect, embodying the archetypal Sage.

Albert Einstein: With his groundbreaking theories and profound insights, Einstein represents the modern Sage, blending deep understanding with a curiosity that changed the world.

Rumi: A 13th-century poet and Sufi mystic, Rumi's work is filled with spiritual wisdom, making him a revered figure who embodies the Sage's deep insights.

Hildegard of Bingen (1098–1179): A medieval Christian mystic, composer, and scholar, Hildegard was a visionary who combined spirituality with science and medicine. She wrote extensively on theology, healing, and the natural world.

Madame Curie: A pioneering scientist, Marie Curie's dedication to research and groundbreaking discoveries in radioactivity define the Sage's pursuit of knowledge and truth.

Professor Minerva McGonagall (*Harry Potter*): McGonagall's strict yet fair guidance at Hogwarts embodies the Sage archetype, blending wisdom with a nurturing spirit.

Morpheus (*The Matrix*): Morpheus, with his deep understanding of the Matrix, acts as a mentor and guide to Neo, symbolizing the Sage's role in revealing deeper truths.

Sojourner Truth (1797–1883): An abolitionist and advocate for women's rights, Truth's wisdom came from lived experience. Her famous speech "Ain't I a Woman?" challenged societal and intellectual arguments about race and gender.

Athena (Greek Mythology): The Greek goddess of wisdom, strategy, and war, Athena represents intellect balanced with action. She serves as a guide to heroes like Odysseus, embodying strategic wisdom.

The Oracle of Delphi (Ancient Greece): As the Pythia, the high priestess of Apollo, the Oracle was revered for her prophetic wisdom, serving as a spiritual guide to leaders and seekers.

Plato (c. 427–347 BCE): The Greek philosopher and student of Socrates, Plato represents the pursuit of wisdom, truth, and justice. His writings, particularly *The Republic*, explore the nature of knowledge and the ideal society. Through dialogues featuring Socrates, he serves as a guide to deeper understanding, shaping Western philosophy and inspiring generations of thinkers.

Appendix B: Symbols and the Alchemy of Leadership

True transformation—whether in leadership or life—isn't merely a process of executing a plan; it's about engaging with the deeper, unseen forces that shape who we are and what we become. By drawing on the wisdom of symbols, myths, and archetypes, we access a map that guides us toward becoming leaders who don't just achieve tasks—they inspire others, initiate meaningful change, and leave an enduring legacy.

The visual elements in this book, designed by Chloe Thompson of Circa Brand Agency, aren't just aesthetic—they're purposeful. They illustrate the profound connection between leadership archetypes and the forces of transformation. Each archetype is linked with a symbol from nature and a crafted object, underscoring the dynamic interplay between instinct and intellect, the wild and the cultivated—essential ingredients for both personal and leadership growth.

Alchemy divides its forces into four elements: Earth, Water, Fire, and Air. These elements tie directly to the leadership archetypes, and here's how it breaks down:

 **Warrior – Fire/Axe:** Fire is all about energy, power, and the transformation that comes from taking on challenges headfirst. The Warrior archetype thrives in this space, using strength and drive to move things forward. The axe, a tool of action, drives this home—symbolizing the raw, decisive power of the Warrior. Fire, in

alchemy, is all about turning the heat up and transforming something tough into something refined and stronger.

Lover – Water/Chalice: Water represents emotion, intuition, and the deep connections that fuel relationships. The Lover archetype is all about empathy and nurturing those connections. The chalice, symbolizing giving and receiving, pairs perfectly with water's fluidity and flow. Just like water adapts and moves, the Lover teaches us how to connect, create, and go with the flow. In alchemy, water is the element of change and emotional depth.

King/Queen – Earth/Castle Tower: Earth stands for stability, structure, and responsibility. That's the King/Queen archetype—grounded, focused on building legacies, and protecting what matters. The castle tower represents strength, protection, and the idea of ruling with wisdom. Earth in alchemy is about creating something solid and long-lasting, much like the leadership of a King or Queen.

Sage – Wind/Book: Wind is about life, clarity, wisdom, and seeing things from a higher perspective. That's the Sage's realm—seeking knowledge and sharing it with others. The book represents learning, insight, and the pursuit of understanding. Wind in alchemy is tied to vision and clarity, giving the Sage the power to guide with calm and wisdom.

Appendix C: Supplemental Reading List

This reading list is here to help you dig deeper into the themes and archetypes we've explored throughout the book. Each book is picked to expand on the insights shared in each chapter. Think of this as a roadmap for further exploration, guiding you to books that will challenge your thinking and offer fresh perspectives. You'll find a mix of classic texts, modern leadership guides, and thought-provoking narratives.

These will help you deepen your understanding of yourself and the leadership qualities you want to cultivate and support you in becoming a more self-aware, effective, and impactful leader.

Introduction and Chapter 1

Archetypes and Personal Growth

King, Warrior, Magician, Lover: Rediscovering the Archetypes of the Mature Masculine by Robert Moore and Douglas Gillette

A seminal work that dives into the core archetypes you explore, making it a perfect foundational text for readers interested in psychological and leadership archetypes.

The Hero with a Thousand Faces by Joseph Campbell

Campbell's classic on mythology and the hero's journey provides a deeper understanding of universal patterns and archetypes in human narratives.

Man and His Symbols by Carl G. Jung

This collection of essays, edited by Jung himself, introduces the concept of archetypes and the role of symbols in the collective unconscious.

Integrating Wisdom Traditions and Leadership:

The Fifth Discipline: The Art and Practice of the Learning Organization by Peter Senge

Offers holistic approach to leadership and systems leadership as an ongoing practice.

The Art of War by Sun Tzu

Although often applied to strategy, this ancient text offers insights into leadership and human nature.

Spiritual and Reflective Leadership:

Let Your Life Speak: Listening for the Voice of Vocation by Parker J. Palmer

Palmer's contemplative exploration of vocation and calling emphasizes self-knowledge and leading from within.

Falling Upward: A Spirituality for the Two Halves of Life by Richard Rohr

Rohr's exploration of the two journeys of life parallels your discussion of the first and second journeys, providing spiritual depth to the leadership journey.

The Road Less Traveled by M. Scott Peck

Combines spirituality, psychology, and leadership.

The Role of Narrative and Storytelling:

The Storytelling Animal: How Stories Make Us Human by Jonathan Gottschall

This book explores why humans are wired for stories and how narratives shape our perception of reality.

The Power of Myth by Joseph Campbell and Bill Moyers

A series of conversations that delve into myth's role in personal and collective meaning-making, providing a framework for understanding how myth shapes leadership and self-understanding.

Chapter 2: The Warrior

Grit: The Power of Passion and Perseverance by Angela Duckworth

Explores the science of perseverance and resilience, showing how these qualities are critical for success and embody the essence of the mature Warrior's strength.

The Obstacle Is the Way: The Timeless Art of Turning Trials into Triumph by Ryan Holiday

Draws on Stoic philosophy to illustrate how embracing hardship can lead to growth and success, mirroring the Warrior's journey through challenges.

The Book of Five Rings by Miyamoto Musashi

A classic text on martial arts and strategy, it delves into the mindset of a warrior, emphasizing discipline, skill, and the mental fortitude needed for victory.

Man's Search for Meaning by Viktor E. Frankl

A profound exploration of finding meaning in suffering, which aligns with the Warrior's quest for purpose amid adversity.

Resilience: Hard-Won Wisdom for Living a Better Life by Eric Greitens

Written by a former Navy SEAL, it offers practical wisdom on resilience, emotional strength, and navigating life's difficulties with the mindset of a modern-day Warrior.

Meditations by Marcus Aurelius

A collection of personal writings by the Stoic philosopher and Roman emperor, focusing on self-discipline, fortitude, and the internal strength required for leadership.

The Warrior Ethos by Steven Pressfield

Examines the code of honor, discipline, and courage that defines the true Warrior, making it a concise and impactful read for understanding the deeper values of this archetype.

Chapter 3: The Lover

The Gifts of Imperfection by Brené Brown

Brené Brown's exploration of vulnerability and wholehearted living is foundational for understanding how embracing imperfections and being open to vulnerability can foster true connection, which lies at the heart of the Lover archetype.

Daring Greatly: How the Courage to Be Vulnerable Transforms the Way We Live, Love, Parent, and Lead by Brené Brown

This book dives into how vulnerability is not a sign of weakness but a source of courage and creativity, encouraging leaders to lead with authenticity and empathy.

The Art of Loving by Erich Fromm

A classic text on the nature of love, Fromm's work explores how love is a skill that must be developed and nurtured. It's an essential read for understanding the Lover's perspective on cultivating deep, reciprocal relationships.

Love in the Time of Cholera by Gabriel García Márquez

This novel beautifully illustrates themes of enduring love, patience, and the complexities of human relationships, resonating deeply with the Lover's journey of connection and vulnerability.

To Bless the Space Between Us: A Book of Blessings by John O'Donohue

A poetic collection of blessings and reflections, O'Donohue's book emphasizes the transformative power of love, kindness, and presence, offering wisdom on how to create spaces where others can feel seen and valued.

Anam Cara: A Book of Celtic Wisdom by John O'Donohue

Drawing on Celtic spirituality, O'Donohue explores themes of soul friendship, beauty, and connection, inviting readers to embrace the Lover's relational approach to life and leadership.

The Five Love Languages: How to Express Heartfelt Commitment to Your Mate by Gary Chapman

This book is a practical guide to understanding different ways of expressing love, helping readers build stronger and more fulfilling relationships—both personal and professional.

Radical Acceptance: Embracing Your Life with the Heart of a Buddha by Tara Brach

Brach's work is a guide to self-compassion, acceptance, and healing, offering practical insights on how to embrace the Lover's energy of empathy and forgiveness in oneself and others.

A Hidden Wholeness: The Journey Toward an Undivided Life by Parker J. Palmer

Palmer's book explores the tension between our inner and outer lives, encouraging leaders to lead from a place of integrity, vulnerability, and compassion—core aspects of the Lover archetype.

The Artist's Way: A Spiritual Path to Higher Creativity by Julia Cameron

This book serves as a practical guide for tapping into the Lover's creative energy. It helps readers explore self-expression, overcome creative blocks, and reconnect with their passion for life.

The Book of Awakening: Having the Life You Want by Being Present to the Life You Have by Mark Nepo

A daily guide that explores the richness of life's experiences, encouraging readers to approach each moment with compassion, openness, and creativity, embodying the essence of the Lover archetype.

Healing Through the Dark Emotions: The Wisdom of Grief, Fear, and Despair by Miriam Greenspan

A guide to understanding and navigating dark emotions with empathy and acceptance, offering a profound look at how grief and heartbreak can be transformative forces in the Lover's journey.

The Prophet by Kahlil Gibran

A timeless classic filled with poetic insights on love, relationships, and the human experience, perfectly capturing the Lover's energy of emotional depth and wisdom.

Chapter 4: The King/Queen

Good to Great: Why Some Companies Make the Leap... and Others Don't by Jim Collins

Explores what makes a company successful in the long term, with a focus on Level 5 Leadership—leaders who combine deep humility with fierce resolve.

Leaders Eat Last: Why Some Teams Pull Together and Others Don't
by Simon Sinek

Focuses on how leaders create environments where people feel safe, empowered, and valued—essential aspects of the King/Queen's role in fostering a healthy, flourishing kingdom.

The Infinite Game by Simon Sinek

Discusses shifting from a finite to an infinite mindset in leadership, emphasizing vision, legacy, and sustainability over short-term gains.

Legacy: What the All Blacks Can Teach Us About the Business of Life by James Kerr

Uses the New Zealand All Blacks rugby team as a case study in leadership, culture, and building legacy, highlighting the King/Queen's responsibility to develop enduring institutions.

The 21 Irrefutable Laws of Leadership: Follow Them and People Will Follow You by John C. Maxwell

Provides foundational principles for effective leadership, such as the Law of Legacy and the Law of Influence, which resonate with the King/Queen's role in guiding others.

The Power of Servant Leadership by Robert K. Greenleaf

Explores the concept of servant leadership, where the King/Queen's true power comes from serving others and lifting them up.

Chapter 5: The Sage

The Art of Living: The Classical Manual on Virtue, Happiness, and Effectiveness by Epictetus

A classic text from Stoic philosophy, offering guidance on cultivating equanimity, self-awareness, and resilience in the face of life's challenges—traits central to the Sage's wisdom.

The Second Mountain: The Quest for a Moral Life by David Brooks

Explores the transition from the pursuit of personal success (the first mountain) to a life of meaning, service, and wisdom (the second mountain), which aligns with the Sage's mature expression.

The Untethered Soul: The Journey Beyond Yourself by Michael A. Singer

A book that invites leaders to explore inner stillness, detachment, and the deeper layers of consciousness, mirroring the Sage's quest for inner peace and understanding.

The Essential Rumi translated by Coleman Barks

A collection of poetry from the 13th-century Sufi mystic, Rumi, whose work embodies the Sage's love for paradox, mystery, and spiritual depth.

The Tao Te Ching by Lao Tzu

A classic guide to the wisdom of the Taoist tradition,

offering insights into balance, humility, and non-attachment—all central to the Sage's posture in leadership.

Zen Mind, Beginner's Mind by Shunryu Suzuki

Explores the importance of maintaining a "beginner's mind," which is open, curious, and humble—key aspects of the Sage's approach to wisdom.

Endnotes

1   The more I worked with these extraordinary people, the more I saw that leaders are asked to navigate crossroads all the time. (So much so that many leaders wind up with decision fatigue, or worse, burned out.) Perhaps one of the clearest distinctions between leadership and followership is the responsibility and willingness to make decisions—especially without all the data.

2   Council Leadership, formerly The Leadership Lab, is a leadership coaching and boutique consultancy based in Nashville with a passion for providing unparalleled personal and professional leadership development for high-character, growth-oriented leaders by focusing on encouraging the heart, shaping the character, and nurturing the growth of leaders and their organizations. We do these three ways: 1) Individual Leadership Development; 2) Organizational and Strategic Leadership Advising; and 3) Thought Leadership.

3   Frameworks help, but none are complete. When you start to look closely, you begin to see archetypal frameworks everywhere. One popular in recent years is the Enneagram, categorizing people into one of nine personalities, each with a specific "type"—e.g., Perfectionist, Achiever, Challenger, etc. There are more scientific personality profiles such as the Culture Index, DISC and Myers-Briggs, as well as other popular assessments like the KOLBE and StrengthsFinder. Each is helpful in certain ways and incomplete in others.

4   Marie-Louise von Franz was a pioneer in Jungian psychology and had this incredible ability to take ancient symbols, alchemy, and mythology, and make them relevant for us today. She didn't just talk about these ideas—she showed us how they can guide us to become who we're meant to be.

Key Insights:

*   Alchemy and Transformation: Von Franz saw alchemy as more than some old, mystical process—it's a metaphor for how we grow and change. The stages of breaking down, refining, and rebuilding mirror the way we face hard truths, grow through

challenges, and come out stronger. Leadership, at its core, is about transformation—both in ourselves and those we lead.

- Fairy Tales and Archetypes: She also showed us that fairy tales and myths aren't just bedtime stories. They're blueprints for life, filled with archetypes that help us understand our own journeys. Whether we're the Warrior, the Lover, the King/Queen, or the Sage, these stories reflect our struggles and our potential to grow into better leaders.

- Working with Carl Jung: Von Franz was one of Jung's closest collaborators, and she helped expand his ideas on individuation—the process of becoming your most authentic self. That's what leadership is, too. It's about owning both your strengths and your shadows, and becoming the kind of leader who's real, vulnerable, and able to inspire others.

- Symbols and Growth: What made von Franz's work stand out is how she connected symbols, mythology, and even dreams to real-world growth. She believed that these symbols aren't just historical relics—they're practical tools for making sense of modern leadership. They help us answer those big questions we all wrestle with: Who am I? What's my purpose? How can I make a real impact?

Key Works:

- *Alchemy: An Introduction to the Symbolism and the Psychology*

- *The Interpretation of Fairy Tales*

- *Psychotherapy*

5 Just as this book is available in its entirety to people of all ages, it is also available to everyone, regardless of gender. Each archetype must be both male and female to be whole. Obviously, this becomes most tricky when we discuss The King/Queen archetype. I considered renaming The King/Queen into a more gender inclusive idea like Monarch, however, there are separate elements to this construct that are helpful in developing our understanding alongside the distinctions of what is most commonly, dependably feminine or masculine.

6   Rohr, Richard. *Falling Upward: A Spirituality for the Two Halves of Life*. San Francisco: Jossey-Bass, 2011.

7   C.G. Jung, *Letters*, Vol1:1906-1950, Bollingen Series XCV:1, Edited by G. Adler & A. Jaffe, Translated by R.F.C. Hull, page 33.

8   The 12 Trials of Heracles

1.   Slaying the Nemean Lion: Heracles strangled the invulnerable lion and wore its hide as armor.

2.   Slaying the Hydra: He defeated the nine-headed serpent by burning its heads as he cut them off.

3.   Capturing the Golden Hind: He captured the swift, sacred deer with golden antlers and bronze hooves.

4.   Capturing the Erymanthian Boar: He trapped the massive boar, showcasing his endurance and tracking skills.

5.   Cleaning the Augean Stables: He diverted rivers to wash out the filth from King Augeas's stables.

6.   Slaying the Stymphalian Birds: He used a rattle from Athena to defeat the man-eating birds with metallic feathers.

7.   Capturing the Cretan Bull: He subdued the bull that terrorized Crete and brought it back alive.

8.   Stealing the Mares of Diomedes: He took the man-eating horses of the Thracian king Diomedes.

9.   Obtaining the Girdle of Hippolyta: He won the magical girdle of the Amazon queen Hippolyta through combat and diplomacy.

10. Obtaining the Cattle of Geryon: He retrieved the cattle of the three-bodied Geryon, overcoming numerous obstacles.

11. Stealing the Apples of the Hesperides: He fetched the golden apples with help from Atlas and his own strength.

12. Capturing Cerberus: His final task was to capture the three-headed guard dog of the Underworld and bring him to the surface.

9   *Oxford Handbook of Heracles*. (n.d.). In Oxford University Press. Retrieved from Oxford Academic (Oxford Academic (https://academic.oup.com/edited-volume/33430/chapter/290585124.)

The Medieval Tradition of Cerberus. (n.d.). In Cambridge University Press. Retrieved from Cambridge Core (Cambridge University Press & Assessment (https://www.cambridge.org/core/journals/traditio/article/medieval-tradition-of-cerberus/F1A542F8C84ACF60F90B3DB5E1C49749.)

Piggott, S. (1938). *The Hercules Myth—Beginnings and Ends.* Antiquity, 12(47), 323-331. Retrieved from Cambridge Core (Cambridge University Press & Assessment. (https://doi.org/10.1017/S0003598X00013946.)

10 James, William. *"The Dilemma of Determinism"* in *The Will to Believe and Other Essays in Popular Philosophy,* 1897.

"Things fade" speaks to the fleeting nature of possibilities, pointing out how moments and options slip away—lost either to the passage of time or the choices we make.

"Alternatives exclude" captures the cost of decision-making: choosing one path means closing the door on others.

Notes